Margarita Palacios

Fantasy and Political Violence

The Meaning of Anti-Communism in Chile

VS RESEARCH

Bibliographic information published by the Deutsche Nationalbibliothek
The Deutsche Nationalbibliothek lists this publication in the Deutsche Nationalbibliografie;
detailed bibliographic data are available in the Internet at http://dnb.d-nb.de.

1st Edition 2009

© VS Verlag für Sozialwissenschaften | GWV Fachverlage GmbH, Wiesbaden 2009

Editorial Office: Dorothee Koch / Anita Wilke

VS Verlag für Sozialwissenschaften is part of the specialist publishing group
Springer Science+Business Media.
www.vs-verlag.de

Cover design: KünkelLopka Medienentwicklung, Heidelberg
Satz: SatzReproService GmbH, Jena
Printed on acid-free paper
Printed in Germany

ISBN 978-3-531-16869-2

Margarita Palacios

Fantasy and Political Violence

VS RESEARCH

Foreword

Since torture is back in the international headlines now, the study by Margarita Palacios "Fantasy and Political Violence" should be required reading. Her book, centered in the analysis of Chilean anticommunism of the early 1970s, analyzes a phenomenon which is difficult to understand: the non-rational side of political violence. We do not yet have studies dealing with the problem as it pertains to the recent history of the United States, aside from massive journalistic revelations and legal investigations concerning what has happened. Among other things, we lack a theoretical analysis such as the one undertaken here by Dr. Palacios. Her focus on Chile is quite salutary because the political institutions, laws, and traditions of Chile before the military coup of 1973 were at least as opposed to what happened during the dictatorship, as U.S. institutions, laws, and traditions were to the admittedly much less violent emergency regime from 2001 to 2008. Thus the question how in a constitutional democracy extreme violence can be possible, can be raised with great advantage in this particular case study.

In my view, the work focuses above all on the imaginary significations that link the underlying agreement of three constituencies in such a way that the massive use of torture as well as disappearances of people in the Chilean case became possible. These three constituencies are the important segments that do the torturing and the killing, the perpetrators, the elites that give the orders, and finally those sectors of the population that accept and even approve of them, at least as far as the elimination of the enemies is concerned. Only the first two segments initially know the facts of torture, but all three know the facts of killing and disappearance reasonably well.

From the point of view of this study, the first category is the most interesting from a psycho-analytical point of view. Only to them does the full Lacanian analysis apply because only they really fully participate in the action and its pleasures. Politically, however, they are the least interesting. As we can now see from the U.S. example, this type of actor today exists in all societies, from Nazi Germany to Israel, from Latin America to India. To some extent, their presence is manifested in police work, especially regarding poor populations who are not well represented and cannot easily respond. But under constitutional normalcy, this type of actor is severely constrained, and its actions belong to the category of a type of official criminality. At certain moments of political exception these actors are unleashed, and this is the work of those who give the orders. There is no question, as we have seen in the United States, that top figures in the executive branch (military officials in Chile) must give the required orders for systematic torture to take place. They know what they are ordering, and all attempts to shift responsibility to subordinates are based on lies. Yet they will not fully participate in the act, and so we must assume that their motivation structure is somewhat different. I think Foucault's analysis of the need to express the plenitude of the monarch's prerogative still holds here, even if Palacios is quite right in pointing to the important difference, namely secrecy, as against the public nature of torture under the old regime. Yet in the leader's community itself, the idea that all this can be done in spite of any law and beyond any punishment must be an important part of motivation. Finally, the most important part of the analysis focuses on the political discourse of large segments of the population in which the image of an absolute enemy was constructed. If it is the goal of the constitutional state to transform enemies into opponents, then the opposite process clearly took place in the period of the Popular Unity government in Chile. Palacios demonstrates the depth and sexual meaning of the relevant imagery, and makes clear that it was quite successful in making disappearance and violence acceptable for a significant segment of Chilean population. This idea is very important to understand the mind-set of the other two categories that were more directly culpable. Being rooted in a community's fears, aspirations and desires are very important for people who are, as Hannah Arendt understood so well, usually totally banal. Torture and disappearance are moreover linked. If a community does not mind that some people simply are done away with then the value of these victims is such that anything whatsoever can be done to them … as the tortures may please.

One should certainly not generalize too far from the Chilean case where the coup of 1973 responded to the possibility of a significant regime change. A comparative analysis would have to disentangle what is universal and what is particular in this case. Its immediate applications will be to the other historical cases of the bureaucratic authoritarian and national security regimes of the 1970s and 1980s. It seems, however, that the theoretical strengths of the analysis of the Chilean case would serve this purpose well also in other contexts that we need to understand if the phenomenon of torture is going to be better constrained than in the last few years.

Andrew Arato

Preface

Accounting for human cruelty it is not an easy task. That is why, as social scientists, we probably find in psychology and political science ways of reducing violence either to individual pathological characteristics or to the interests of groups who aim to achieve or retain power. Both of these tendencies mean that we do not really have to confront the physicality and pain of violence, and most importantly, they also free us from our ethical responsibility – 'they' committed the crimes or are responsible for them, 'we' are not. In this research I have taken a different perspective. The horror and abuse that characterize the testimonies of torture survivors proved – early on in my research – that traditional accounts of political violence fall short in understanding this phenomenon. Although it was often possible to see the underlying strategy, most of the time it just seemed as though violence exceeded any rational purpose and had no other aim than to destroy the humanity and dignity left in an already broken body. Moreover, the significant and active support that wide sectors of Chilean society gave to the emerging Junta in 1973, and the silence and willingness to ignore the human right abuses that were committed in the country during the military regime, point to the participation not only of particular individuals willing to commit the crimes, but of a society that supported the repressive regime.

Inspired by the psychoanalytical concept of fantasy, I argue in this book that the violence that emerged in Chile after the military coup of 1973 is related to a wider socio-cultural process of fear and hatred, in which violence not only aimed to repress left-wing political activists, but also to 'extirpate from the Chilean soul' a devil that was destroying the nation, to punish a society for having allowed this to happen, and to restore a patriarchal social order. The concept of fantasy has also allowed me to understand the paradoxical dynamic of morality and enjoyment that characterized political violence in Chile, which was justified as a moral calling to rescue society from evil, but at the same time involved a perverse eroticization of death.

This approach does not absolve the individuals who participated in the orchestration or execution of violence of responsibility and authorship. However, it does question the role of Chilean civil society in the emergence of political antagonism and in its violent outcome.

London, 2009   Margarita Palacios

Contents

Introduction

Villa Grimaldi:

"The most common torture method was electrical shock, consisting of a metal rack to which the naked prisoner was tied and then electrical current would be applied to different parts of his or her body, especially the most sensitive areas such as the lips or genitals or even on wounds or metallic prostheses. One particularly cruel variation of this method consisted in further pressuring the subject of interrogation by placing him on the bottom rack of a double bunk bed and torturing a family member or friend above him. Another torture method often employed was hanging. The victim was hung from a bar, either by the wrists or by wrists and ankles. In both cases, the pain produced over time by the weight of the hanging body, was aggravated by applying electrical shocks, beatings, penetrating wounds and other types of aggravation. Submerging the person's head in a container of water – usually dirty – or some other liquid was another torture method often used at Villa Grimaldi. The victim's head would be held underwater almost until the point of asphyxiation. A similar effect was obtained through the so-called 'dry submarine', which consisted in placing a plastic bag around the person's head to prevent him or her from breathing. In addition to those methods already described, which were the most common some agents occasionally employed other techniques. There are testimonies stating that on one occasion, in the case of the Gallardo family... boiling water or other liquid was thrown on various prisoners as a method of punishment and in anticipation of their eventual death."

(http://www.chipsites.com/derechos/campo_santiago_villa_ grimaldi_eng.html)

The National Stadium:

"Every night we would hear the screams of the workers who were executed in the east wing of the National Stadium in Santiago. The next day, the blood stains were washed away with hoses. Everyday, observers would see a pile of shoes that had been worn by the victims of the previous night. Between September 12 and 13, the National Stadium was turned into what would be the largest detention camp in Santiago. The Red Cross International estimates there were about 7,000 prisoners there as of September 22, and 200 to 300 of those were not Chilean citizens. The army controlled the National Stadium and brought in prisoners from all over Santiago. The National Stadium prisoners slept in the locker rooms and in the tower room, both places without beds. The women's areas did have sleeping mats. Some charitable international organizations subsequently donated blankets, which were in any case insufficient for the large number of people confined there. The prisoners were held incommunicado, without authorization to receive visits from family members or lawyers, or any outside person. Prisoners' families were only allowed to take them clothing and food."

(http://www.chipsites.com/derechos/campo_santiago_estadio_ nacional_eng.html)

Colonia Dignidad:

> *"In February, 1975, a young medical student named Luis Peebles spent nine days in Colo-*
> *nia Dignidad. His testimony, along with that of other survivors and a former agent of the*
> *Chilean secret police, formed the basis of reports by Amnesty International, the United Na-*
> *tions and other human rights organizations that accused Colonia Dignidad of functioning*
> *as a prison camp and centre for training and experimentation with torture techniques, after*
> *the 1973 military coup: 'My body was full of cuts and bruises. I was rotting everywhere. I*
> *had pus in my eyes, my nose. My mouth was completely numb. I could feel nothing in my*
> *penis and I couldn't feel my limbs. My body was full of cigarette burns'. 'They tied me to a*
> *metal cot, but this time they put a helmet on my head. It had movable earflaps which al-*
> *lowed them to apply electrical current to my ears and rubber bands for around the jaw.*
> *This was so that when they kicked or punched me, my jaw wouldn't get thrust out of joint.*
> *They taped little wires to my wrists, thighs, glands, chest, neck and applied current in dif-*
> *ferent parts. There was also an agent who used a little rubber object which gave off shocks*
> *when he hit me with it. They had something they used on my eyes, mouth, teeth, under my*
> *tongue and sometimes, when I was shouting, they'd put it right at the back of the palate. I*
> *had another one in my anus, at the base of the urethra and another under my nails... This*
> *went on for hours and hours. ... The pain was so great that I twisted and several times lifted*
> *up the bed. I even bent the cot which was of iron and broke the straps with the strength of*
> *desperation."*

(http://www.chipsites.com/derechos/ testimonio_dignidad_2_eng.html)

> *"A woman describes the corpse of her son, the manager of a state cement plant, who turned*
> *himself in after the coup and died in custody five weeks later: 'He was missing one eye, his*
> *nose was torn off, one ear was separated and hanging, there were marks of deep burns on*
> *his neck and face, his mouth was very swollen'."*[1]

Villa Grimaldi, the National Stadium and Colonia Dignidad were only three out of the 1,132 detention centers which were established all around the country after the military coup in Chile. The Chilean democratic tradition had vanished behind an immense repressive apparatus which kept the country captive until 1990. Arbitrary arrest, imprisonment, torture, forced disappearances, summary executions, collective executions, denial of the right to appeal War Council sentences, homicide, exile, internal exile, abduction, intimidation, attempted homicide, death threats, raids, dismissal from jobs and surveillance were the most common types of human rights violations that characterized the entire military regime. The Rettig Report and the National Commission for Reconciliation and Reparation[2] concluded in 1996 that a total of 3,197 people died or went missing between September 11 1973 and March 11 1990 as the result of human rights violations at the hands of the state agents of re-

---

[1] Report of Chilean National Commission on Truth and Reconciliation, 1993. Cited by www.remember-chile.org.uk.

[2] Truth Commissions Digital Collection: Reports: Chile at http://www.usip.org/library/tc/ doc/reports/chile/.

pression. The commission that investigated political prison and torture[3] in Chile established that 27,255 persons suffered torture (1080 detainees at the time were younger than 18 years old).

1 The Interpretations

How could this type of violence emerge so fiercely in a country with a modern lifestyle and a consolidated democratic tradition? With the salience of the cold war's anti-communist rhetoric, direct United States support in the overthrow of the socialist regime in Chile and the simultaneous emergence of military dictatorships in the southern cone against previous populist regimes, the explanation offered by political scientists became hegemonic. In their view the Chilean case corresponded to one more example of well known bureaucratic military regimes, and therefore, its violence was typified as *strategic*: violence and the production of fear in the population aimed at the dismantling of political activity and the production of political apathy, to allow the military to govern without opposition. Thus defined, violence remained a residual, though constitutive, category of military regimes. As a phenomenon in itself – with its own logic – it remained unexplored.

Studies on public violence that emphasize either the state and the rational organization of collective action (Tilly, 1978), or the psychological factors related to social structural transformations (Dollard, Miller & Doob, 1939; Gurr, 1970; Smelser, 1962), allow us to understand only partially the phenomenon of violence: as the analysis of the Chilean case shows, neither frustration nor rationality alone can account for the violence that emerged after the coup. Studies of violence inspired by a cultural perspective (Swider, 1995; Poole, 1994; Wood, 2003), on the other hand, allow a better grasp of the complexity of the phenomenon while considering many of the variables related to violence (such as the subjective process that accompanies it and the power relations that are at play). However, most of the time, such accounts tend to be ethnographic and therefore do not offer a theoretical argument where all the elements present in the expression of collective violence are integrated and explained. Most importantly, their analysis leaves out the dimension of desire and enjoyment, which I find crucial for understanding the hatred that characterizes violence.

When the physicality of violence is at the center of the analysis, however, it soon becomes clear that the rational-strategic interpretation offers only the tip of the ice-

---

[3] www.justiceinperspective.org.

berg of a much deeper social process. In fact, while it is often possible to identify the strategy of violence (characterized by clear and efficient violent means of action, a rational organization of a repressive apparatus, a political aim of the group seizing power), it is also possible to see that violence has not always sought a political goal. Violence perpetrated against children is the best and most tragic illustration of this phenomenon. The use of physical violence against an enemy who has already surrendered, the excess and cruelty in the torture of prisoners, and the mutilation of their bodies (which were later concealed and not publicly displayed) show that it is not always rationality that motivates violence.

2   A Divided Society: Thirty-three Years later

The death of the Chilean former dictator Augusto Pinochet Ugarte, a quiet summer Sunday afternoon in Santiago, opened the Pandora's Box that Chilean society has attempted to keep far from sight once more. As the disruptive events following the death of Pinochet showed, Chilean society has not yet reached an agreement about the meaning of the bloody coup of 1973 and the 17-year military regime that followed it. As hundreds of people gathered in downtown Santiago to celebrate 'the death of the dictator', crowds uptown at the Military Hospital, where Pinochet lay dead after a congestive heart failure, mourned 'the death of the savior' of the country. The abyss that divided Chilean society in 1973 still divided it in 2006. As commented in the media: "Despite Pinochet's human rights record, many Chileans loved him and said he saved Chile from Marxism. But even many loyal supporters abandoned him after it emerged in 2004 that he had stashed some $27m in secret offshore bank accounts that were under investigation at the time of his death."[4]

Institutionally, this divide between *pinochetistas* and *anti-pinochetistas* followed a similar pattern. The decades of attempting to bring Pinochet to justice died with the death of the general. Diplomatic immunity and health reasons prevented Pinochet from facing trial on several occasions.

Sociologists and political scientists, on the other hand, have found neither a consensus regarding the meaning of the breakdown of democracy nor the violence that followed it. Initial discussions in the late seventies questioned whether the key variable was to be found in the economic crisis that preceded the coup or whether it was more a political phenomenon in its own right.

---

[4] http://news.sky.com/skynews/Home/Sky-News-Archive/Article/20080641243577.

The first perspective is best known as O'Donnell's model of bureaucratic military regimes. According to several authors that contributed to the volume *The New Authoritarianism in Latin America* (Collier, 1980), the process of modernization in Latin America produced an impasse firstly between the activated popular sector, i.e. the beneficiaries of populist economic distribution; secondly, the governing political alliances caught between the pressure of the electorate and the growing fiscal deficit; and thirdly, the technocrats. The last of these was a new social actor which emerged precisely out of the modernization process but saw no alternative for further modernization in the populist regimes. From this last group, O'Donnell argues, the different coup coalitions which later governed the different countries, and which inaugurated in all of them a clear 'post-populist' era emerged.

Juan Linz and Alfred Stepan (1978) and Arturo Valenzuela (1978) put forward the political thesis. According to them, it was possible to see in every breakdown the peculiar political crisis that made further political negotiation impossible. In Chile's case, this meant that the replacement of the pragmatic center by an ideological center and the politicization of otherwise non-political actors, such as the military and the judiciary, lead to the breakdown of democracy. These perspectives certainly do not contradict each other, they simply put the accent on different parts of the equation.

The disclosure of CIA files (Kornbluh, 2003) made a significant contribution to clarifying the events. Although it was always clear that in 1954 the U.S. had already orchestrated a coup against Guatemalan reformist Jacobo Arbenz and that all the Latin American breakdowns took place in the context of the cold war, the availability of concrete information about the economic, professional and military involvement of the U.S. government made the analysis of the picture yet more complex and the apportioning of responsibilities more uncertain.

Today, fingers are being pointed in every direction. The first to be blamed are the populists and revolutionaries. Given our current market-oriented political culture, populist economic measures are seen as having brought countries to chaos and to economic disaster. In this view, the anti-systemic rhetoric and behavior of the revolutionaries broke an existing political consensus and destroyed public institutions.

The other main culprit is the military. Their violent acts and abuses of human rights have become known and morally condemned through the publications of truth commissions in each country. Fingers are also being pointed at the people responsible for U.S. interventions in efforts to overthrow democratic regimes.

The writings of historians, journalists, political scientists and sociologists have given us a detailed panorama of the economic, political and social conflicts that were at stake in the breakdowns of democracy in Latin America. Indeed, so much has been written and discussed and so many facts are available to the public that one wonders if there is some piece of the story still missing. I venture to say there is. To understand the emergence and permanence of a violent regime in a country like Chile, characterized by its political stability and its strong democratic culture, one needs to investigate the role of civil society. Broad parts of the population formed a supporting, if not necessarily active, public for the Pinochet coup. More than making a judgment about its political role, one needs to analyze the structure of meaning of anti-communism that pervaded civil society during the three years of Salvador Allende's government which preceded the coup.

My thesis is that anti-communism changed dramatically in those years. It went from a particular kind of political discourse against a particular political program in 1970 to become a condensed expression of generalized anxiety about the viability of life and meaning as a whole in 1973. This displacement of meaning was accompanied by another fundamental transformation. The enemy was no longer the militant of a leftist political party, but a society that had been poisoned by the seeds of 'amoral communism'. Youth and children alike had been exposed and contaminated. What is interesting to stress here is that this society was both victim and perpetrator. It was its own fault that it had become 'communist', and now it needed to be 'saved' and 'punished' or 'saved while punished'. Without attempting to provide a causal explanation, I would suggest that the violence after the coup is related to this re-signification process.

The interpretation I offer in this book widens the existing interpretation of the breakdown of democracy in Chile while putting the local social and cultural dynamic which accompanied the broader regional political process at the center of analysis. My purpose is to show that though there was a shared regional anti-communist doctrine that inspired all the military regimes in the southern cone during the seventies, the specific meaning of anti-communism was locally defined; each country fought a different enemy, and therefore each fight was different. The reason is very simple: not only were political actors and political culture different, but the social milieu also varied from country to country. For Chile, as I have already suggested, anti-communism was the crystallization of a deep cultural and social dynamic of fear and hatred: fear of social disintegration – associated with the feminization of Chilean society – and hatred against disavowed aspects of Chilean identity. The brutality of the violence not only aimed to repress left-wing political activists, but to 'extirpate from the Chilean soul' a devil that was destroying the nation, to punish a society for having allowed this to happen, and to restore a patriarchal social order. The mixture of horror and excitement that characterized the pre-coup Chilean press points to the participation (albeit not necessarily hands on) of civil society in the emergence of violence, and also to the paradoxical dynamic of morality and enjoyment that characterized it: violence was justified as a moral calling to rescue society from evil, but at the same time it involved a perverse eroticization of death.

3   Theory of Violence

It is for this reason that in the book I undertake the task of sketching an outline of a theory of violence, which theorizes violence from the perspective of identity construction and the limits of integrating the *other* within it. This new approach will give me the necessary conceptual tools to do both: understand the universal/structural logic of violence and the particular/local process of symbolic construction of an enemy in Chile. This book presents a gender-based, informed, cultural, theoretical and historical interpretation of the symbolic construction of the communist as the enemy of the country, which is mostly overlooked by studies on political violence. I start by arguing that the lack of a comprehensive theory of violence is related to the fact that, except in Durkheim, social theory has not conceptualized radical otherness as a basic component of social life. The radical other is not the 'different other' with whom understanding and reciprocity is possible, but the un-reachable other, the other with whom there is no communication, the other that threatens the very existence of the self. This lack of conceptualization of the radical other has meant a poor understanding of the relation of enmity that characterizes violence. In my view, only by analyzing the relation between the (violent) *self* and the (enemy) *other* can we understand what violence is about. Although the understanding of the relation between the self and the other has been at the very center of social theory, otherness has been conceptualized so far as always potentially 'subsumed' by the sameness of the self. The self is portrayed as always being able to assimilate the other within itself. Again, social theorists have not overlooked the other, but they have actively attempted to get rid of it. The three existing paradigms for the interpretation of violence are built, in fact, on these types of premises. Relying on structural functionalist theories (violence as breakdown), on Marxist/rationalist theories (strategic violence), or on cultural approaches (identity, power and violence) – though with different arguments and for different reasons – they all agree that the presence of the *other* represents a failure of a self who has not been able to tame it adequately. This is because most of the time theories are normative: violence is always considered an exceptional moment in social life, and is never related to an intrinsic rupture between the self and the other.

On the contrary, I argue here that violence is constitutive of our society as far as it is the expression of a necessary act of exclusion that takes place in the process of the

constitution of the social identity. This means that an antagonistic relationship is established in the process of identity formation between the identity and what needs to
be excluded from it for the identity to exist (Laclau & Mouffe, 1985). This first foundational act of exclusion is cast in positive terms by a transcendental narrative about
the identity, which Castoriadis called 'the social imaginary' (Castoriadis, 1998).
Since the stability of the identity relies on such an exclusion, any threat to the boundary of the identity, from within or without, enacts a (probably violent) response from
the identity against the apparent cause of its instability. The transcendental narrative
provides the identity with the 'moral legitimacy' to attack what threatens it and restore social order. The claim about the *constitutive outsider* comes not only from philosophy (Culler, 1982; Dews, 1995) and psychoanalysis (Elliot, 2002; Fink, 2000),
but from sociology itself (Durkheim 1965, 1984).

By taking a different perspective from the one used by crowd behavior theorists, I
want to recover the non-rational/non-social (neither strategic nor learnt) component
of violence, and discover its internal logic and meaning. I do so by using the Lacanian notion of fantasy as presented in the work of Zizek (1989, 1994, 1997). Fantasy
plays a crucial role in the constitution of the social identity and it seems to dissolve
the previous existing dichotomy in the literature of violence; meaning/rationality vs.
irrationality. Fantasy provides the identity with a transcendental narrative: an idea of
wholeness which conceals the inconsistency – and arbitrariness – of the formation of
the social and contributes to the stability of a particular system of meaning. The transcendental narrative about the identity is also a narrative about the apparent cause of
its instability; a narrative about a pernicious other is also constructed.

However, it is possible to go one step further and state that public violence (at least
in modern societies) not only seeks the restoration of social order, but the restoration
– or reinforcement – of masculine law or patriarchal social order. Such social order is
organized around a particular mode of enjoyment *(phallic jouissance)* as a particular
form of transgressing the law. Violence and exclusion will be regarded in my book as
expressions of a masculine way of enjoying the transgression of the symbolic order,
and paradoxically, as ways of restoring such an order. In this framework, the excluded other *par excellence* is feminine desire, associated in our masculine culture with
passivity and disintegration.

4   The Use of Psychoanalytical Theory

Let me add a few words in order to explain why the use of psychoanalysis appears
pertinent for my study. First of all, psychoanalysis not only theorizes the rupture

self/other, but also gives us elements to understand the physicality of violence which existing theories do not account for. The relation with the enemy, as we will see later, is characterized by aggressive jealousy or jealousy of enjoyment, where the other is seen as somebody who prevents or steals enjoyment from the self. Additionally, the enjoyment of the other's suffering is constitutive of (excessive) violence. Psychoanalytical theory will provide us with elements to understand this complex dynamic.

Secondly, Lacan (1977, 1978, 1998) solves a problem that social theory was incapable of resolving, namely, the simultaneous theorization of power and separation from power (or resistance). Social theory has either over-theorized agency (rationalistic and interpretative approaches) or determination (functionalism and structuralism). In the first case the subject is a free agent acting according to its will, in the second the subject belongs to the symbolic order. Lacan, on the contrary, acknowledges the omniscience of power (expressed in the internalization of the symbolic order and in the parallel evacuation of enjoyment) but at the same time does not reduce the subject to this process of subjectivation. Lacan states that beyond (or prior to) the historical process of social formation of the subject, there is a space of being which is not retrievable by language and, as such, does not manifest itself in a meaningful or coherent way. On the contrary, it appears as a disruption of the symbolic order (as a 'symptom'). Therefore, although Lacan certainly accepts the social nature of the subject, he still defends a strong notion of subjectivity. Contrary to the self-aware and transparent subject of the Cartesian *cogito*, and contrary to the empty space that is filled (normalized) with discourses, the space of subjectivity in the case of Lacan is a space which contains what the subject is but that, at the same time, represents its impossibility. The concept of 'beyond language' – the 'beyond the social' – is denominated as the 'real', expressed in the remnants of an incomplete process of symbolization. This is *jouissance*, or pure pulsing drive.

Defining this space of pure being, of lack of symbolization, Lacan is able to draw an unconscious as a 'radical other' which cannot be retrieved through any process of communication.

Thirdly, the use of psychoanalytical theory will allow us to see that the radical other which threatens the self is nothing but an aspect of the self which needs to be repressed (excluded/abjected) for the self to emerge. The self is not complete or coherent, but split, divided, alienated. Its own foundation is based on a negation, and its survival on the perpetuation of such negation (through repression). This dynamic will help us to understand the emergence of violence and its excess, when enacted against members of one's own community. As we will see later, violence emerges when the identity as such is threatened; when the other is seen as being able to uncover the thin veil that covers what is being repressed. In such cases, the other is invested with what the self (unconsciously) fears about itself. The self projects onto the other what it represses in itself.

There is one last question regarding the use of psychoanalytical theory. Is the individual self equal to the social self? Quite obviously it is not. However, the works of Durkheim (1965, 1984), Freud (1950, 1959, 1961), Lacan (1977, 1978), Castoriadis (1996, 1998), Laclau & Mouffe (1985), and Zizek (1989, 1994, 1997) have shown both the existence of a similar logic in the constitution of every social identity and their mutual belonging. As products of language, it could be argued, social identities share a similar identity structure. The fact that Lacan 'translated' Freudian psychoanalysis to the language of linguistic structuralism makes the transition and interaction between individual selves and social selves very smooth: they are both 'sewn' by the signifying operation of language. In other words, the use of psychoanalytical theory will allow us to understand the nature of the social bond Durkheim described as being constitutive of society. It is therefore incorrect to equate psychoanalytical theory to individual psychology. As will become clearer, the Lacanian subject is *'neither the individual nor the conscious subject of analytical philosophy'*, but the split/barred subject of the unconscious. The notion of the 'divided subject' is the concept with which psychoanalysis distances itself from every form of psychology.

At the same time it is also incorrect to assume that the use of psychoanalytical theory involves departing from a theory of the subject and extrapolating it to the social in a more or less arbitrary movement. On the contrary, Lacanian psychoanalysis is a theory about the impossible relation between language (the symbolic order) and being (the real, or what escapes symbolization). It is a theory about desire as the difference that remains after a (felt) need is translated (through language) into a demand, about the different positions subjects can take regarding this unsatisfied desire, and, finally, about the way society masks this fissure between language and being (through the game of fantasies).

Summing up, the tri-partite Lacanian register of the Symbolic, the Imaginary and the Real, describes the nature and limits of the symbolic order (described as 'perforated' by being), and the way subjects belong and evade/resist it. Therefore, the use of clinical notions by Lacan should not be interpreted as attempting to 'stigmatize' a patient, but as ways of describing different positions the subject can take regarding this impossibility. The best example of this is sexuality itself: masculinity and femininity describe two different ways of 'failing within language'.

5   Methodology

Agreeing with Habermas (1962), Chilean scholars have recognized the central role of the press during the period 1970-73 in the creation of a Chilean public opinion and of counterpublics in general (Sunkel, 1983; Duran, 1995; Reyes Matta & Ruiz, 1989). Not that the press really helped in the construction of a rational public sphere, but it certainly both expressed the existing level of anxiety and psychological regression of the population and became a fundamental element in the reproduction and increase of such anxiety (Durán, 1995).

Using Sunkel's (1983) distinction between 'enlightened' newspapers (those that understand rationality as a means of mutual understanding and progress as the goal of history), and 'symbolic-dramatic' newspapers (those that reject rationality, use concrete rather than abstract language, and are based on religious conceptions of the world), I analyzed one newspaper for each genre: El Mercurio (for the first one) and Tribuna (for the second). El Mercurio is the oldest Chilean newspaper (founded in 1900), and its target is the enlightened Chilean public. The newspaper Tribuna, on the other hand, was the expression of the radicalized right-wing, whose aim with the newspaper was to 'fight communism, the enemy of Chile'. Though this newspaper only existed for two years (1972–1973), it was a main part of the news media during the socialist government.

The methodology I used was inspired by Salecl's use of French linguistics (Salecl, 1996). She distinguishes the presence of three elements in a discourse: the *present discourse*, the *later discourse* and the *surmise*. The first refers to the actual content of what it is said; the second to the wider symbolic framework that organizes the speech; and the third to the way the addressee must decipher the meaning of what was said. The present and the later discourse belong to the realm of meaning; the surmise refers to the realm of fantasy. Salecl states that contrary to speech acts theory (Austin, 1962) – where the subject's intention matches the speech act itself – discourse analysis must acknowledge the impossibility of full recognition, and the presence instead of a space or blank, a margin of doubt about the other's desire.

Though usually the press is considered as a medium for *propaganda* (the rational-strategic action of individuals in pursuit of a political goal through the use of media), I selected the press coverage of the electoral campaigns as my focus of analysis because it seems to be a good medium to analyze fantasies. According to Kristeva (1980, 1984), the signifying process involves both, a *symbolic* and a *semiotic-chora* modalities. The first one refers to the realm of signification and it presupposes a constituted-conscious subject. The second one refers instead to the articulation of drives, and presupposes a de-centered subject. According to her, the symbolic and semiotic are always present in language, and the dialectic between them determines the type of discourse involved (poetry, science, narrative, etc.). The polymorphous character of the press (the combination of genres such as news, pictures, editorials, headlines, cartoons, etc.) seems to combine both symbolic and semiotic modalities neatly. The press not only provides the open and strategic position of the right and its political culture (its wider symbolic framework), but also allows us to read between the lines about how the right constructed its fantasies about the left.

I interpreted fantasies (or the latent content of the discourse) based on the psycho-analytical theory of signifying substitution. In *The Interpretation of Dreams* (1965) Freud distinguishes between the manifest and latent content of dreams, and comparing them he introduced the notions of *condensation* and *displacement*. The first one explains the process of unification of different things or elements into a single one, and the second, the process of substitution of elements carried out during the process of formation of the dream. Jacques Lacan suggested that condensation and displacement could be equated to the speech figures of metaphor and metonymy. A metaphor involves a signifying substitution. This means that a signifier (a concept) that is usually associated to a particular signified (meaning) is associated, this time, to a different meaning.

Metaphors communicate meaning by analogy, by explaining or interpreting one thing in terms of something else, and they carry out a process of selection. In the case of metonymy, there is a signifier substitution, which means that a signified (or meaning), which is usually associated to a particular signifier (or concept), is associated this time, to a different concept (Dor, 1997). In this speech figure meaning is communicated by association (not by selection) and involves a process of combination.

6   Organization of the Book

The book is divided in two parts. In the first part I present the theory and in the second part, the case study. My argument in the first part is that social theory has not conceptualized radical otherness, which is why sociological and political accounts on violence remain partial and most of the time ignore the physicality of violence altogether. Based on the notions of hegemony and fantasy, I develop an alternative outline for understanding the relation of antagonism which characterizes violence. I present the notion of sexual difference as a starting point for critical analysis of violence in our patriarchal societies.

Through a survey of major exponents of social theory (such as American functionalism, Marxism, symbolic interactionism and post-structuralism), in chapter 1, I show how social thought, though always concerned with the other, has failed to theorize radical otherness – the other is ultimately understood as always being subsumed by the sameness of the self. This lack of conceptualization has led to a partial understanding of the phenomenon of violence. Through reading Durkheim, Schmitt, Laclau and Lacan, in chapter 2 I argue that social antagonism and its violent expression cannot be understood if social theory does not conceptualize radical otherness as the pre-condition of society. Moreover, I argue that only by adding the category of enjoyment (pleasure derived from transgression), can we begin to grasp what violence is about. Violence is related to the fear of symbolic disintegration and is enacted against the group that is perceived to cause such a threat. I present the notion of fantasy to describe the arbitrary symbolic construction of the other and the enjoyment of its exclusion.

Chapter 3 aims to show that collective violence not only seeks the restoration of social order, but the restoration – or reinforcement – of a *masculine law* or patriarchal social order. In this framework the excluded other *par excellence* is feminine desire, associated in our masculine culture with passivity and disintegration. Departing from the Freudian and Lacanian notion of sexual difference, I argue that masculinity and femininity inform different relations with otherness. Because of the fear of castration, masculinity accounts for the logic of exclusion and violence. Not being threatened by castration, nor entirely bound by the symbolic, femininity, on the other hand, accounts for the logic of inclusion. Furthermore, I argue that this feminine logic could be paralleled to the religious experience of dualism (and not to sublimation, as often stated). Thus defined, femininity, though not entirely destabilizing the social order, provides the impetus for its questioning and transformation. In Chapter 4, I present the notion of hegemony and discuss the relation between democracy, social antagonism and violence. How can the political arrangement of a society foster or prevent social antagonism? The answer is through an open public sphere which recognizes both: the impossibility of full inclusion (therefore it is permanently aware of the existing power relations) and the very physicality of social relations (which means acknowledging the relation of 'aggressive jealously' that characterizes social antagonism). I develop this argument through a critical reading of Habermas and Laclau. I address the inadequacy and danger of making universal ethical claims of the first approach, and though I sympathize with the second, I criticize its disembodied and existential character.

In chapter 5 I define the key elements that are present in a relation of antagonism that leads to violence. I argue that a violent fantasy is characterized by the presence of four elements: universality, antagonism, sexuality and hate.

In the second part of the book I present the discourse analysis following the logic described earlier in the methodology section. I start by presenting the 'later discourse' – the symbolic framework that oriented the political right and left during the 20th century. Then I introduce the 'present discourse' of the propaganda of the political right during the three years before the coup, and I finish with an analysis of the 'surmise', where I offer an interpretation of the meaning of anti-communism in Chile during the early seventies. Throughout these chapters I show how the signifier 'communism' is gradually emptied of its ideological-political signification and how new chains of equivalencies are created. This transformation, rather than political, I argue, is a social-cultural transformation. The 'enemy' of the country, though represented as the communist, actually refers to something wider and more abstract, therefore all the more dangerous; the soul of the country has been poisoned. Chapter 6 explores the political identities of the right and the left in Chile and how their different self-definitions and definitions of the other allowed them to either remain reformist or become revolutionary. I analyze how, though inspired by revolutionary doctrines, the left remained mostly in a reformist position, while the conservative right was able to become revolutionary (and violent) in the early seventies. In chapter 7, I present a detailed analysis of how the two right-wing newspapers El Mercurio and Tribuna portrayed the left during the months that surrounded the presidential and parliamentary elections of 1970 and 1973. I show that the constitutive elements of a relation of antagonism grew and defined themselves clearly during the three years of Salvador Allende's socialist government.

In chapter 8, I offer my interpretation of the meaning of anti-communism. I argue that anti-communism in Chile represented a variety of fears and hates. The first and most obvious was the opposition to the structural economic changes pursued by the socialist government. A second, and greater fear, was that of anomie. The legalist, orderly, friendly and rational country in the early seventies had turned into a passionate, chaotic and hateful place. The social, economic and political chaos that had been experienced in the country since the late sixties, though initially seen as the product of bad political leadership, was later perceived as the consequence of an amoral public: the people of Chile had become a sinister monster capable of the worst crimes committed to satisfy their basest passions. I argue that the displacement of hate from the left-wing political elites to the general public is crucial in understanding the spread and character of the violence that occurred in 1973. The political fight (and subsequent repression) was not only against an imaginary well-organized 'red army' but a fight against a 'Frankenstein', or malevolent Chilean spirit, which had been awakened by the socialist government.

First Part:

Understanding Political Violence

Chapter 1: Otherness in Social Theory

In this introductory chapter I present some of the most relevant contributions of so-cial theory to the understanding of the emergence of the self and its relation to the 'other'. As we will see in what follows, social thought, although always concerned with the other, has failed to theorize radical otherness; the other has been ultimately understood as always being subsumed by the sameness of the self. This lack of con-ceptualization of radical otherness has resulted in rather poor understandings of the phenomenon of violence; violence has been understood as an exceptional moment of society (and not as a permanent-constitutive process of construction of other-ness). At the same time, the very physicality that characterizes violence has more of-ten than not been left out of the picture. Aggression has only been theorized from a psychological perspective (Dollard, Miller & Doob, 1939; Gurr, 1970).

Theories of the self can be divided into three different frameworks according to the weight they assign to the process of social determination that society exercises over the subject, and the level (or capacity) of agency they recognize in it. Absolute social determination and complete agency correspond respectively to the extremes of a continuum where the subject is seen either as determined by his environment (without any capacity of creating or acting by himself) or as autonomous from his environment and acting according to his will (or reason). The first approach (social determination) corresponds to normative or functionalist theories of action, which assume that it is possible for the subject to reach a complete process of socialization. According to this framework, the individual acts according to pre-established social roles which exert an influence as moral imperatives (Parsons, 1937, 1951). The sec-ond approach (total agency) is represented by what are termed utilitarian theories or rational choice theory (Olson, 1968, Elster, 1989). According to rational theory au-thors, the individual is an autonomous subject, capable of exercising his will and choosing the course of his action rationally. Contrary to the normative explanation of action, in rational choice theory, the individual possesses full agency, and regardless of the context, his action always expresses the same preference and intention: maxi-mization of utilities.

Most social theorists, however, develop accounts of action which occupy a middle ground. The subject is theorized as the result of the incorporation of the symbolic and cultural patterns of society, but is still regarded as being an active agent. Theories of ideology, post-structuralism, and interpretative approaches in general, share this basic understanding. Though in all of them otherness means something different, ultimately in all of these accounts the other can be, or should be, assimilated by the self. Let us look more closely into these approaches.

1   The 'Deviant' Other

In *The Structure of Social Action* (1937) Parsons presented a new synthetic model of interrelation between social structure and action, where human action was conceived as the result of the enactment of supra-individual norms, and the enactment of individuality. Later on, in *The Social System* (1951) Parsons developed a threefold theory where he incorporated the concepts of personality, culture and society, as the main dimensions involved in the process of socialization. Under the influence of Freud's writing, Parsons argued that individuals have the need (or capacity) to identify with external discourses, making them their own identities. During the process of socialization the individual acquires social knowledge and makes it his own life.

Parsons also stated that social roles are impersonal social niches that can be performed by any individual, and that they refer to the obligation to act according to the position an individual occupies in society. Perfect socialization takes place when the social role coincides with both individual aspirations and society's demands and offers. "Perfect institutionalization occurs when role demands from the social system complement cultural ideals and when both, in turn, meet the needs of the personality. In other words, what the personality needs, in the ideal case, should be the same as what the culture views as meaningfully significant, and these in turn, should be matched by the resources the social system has provided for what it defines as appropriate role obligations. If there is perfect harmony between the different levels of society, individual interaction will be complementary and conflict will not occur." (Alexander, 1987, p. 47.)

In the light of this theory, the other is a deviant. Deviant behavior is the material result of badly adapted individuals, due either to their own personal characteristics, or to problems in the process of socialization itself. In order to prevent deviance, society should tend to the perfection of its socialization system, which is carried out particularly through education, making it possible to match personality, values and social needs.

Parsonian studies on collective behavior elaborated quite conservative accounts of social movements (Smelser, 1962). They were understood in terms of breakdowns due to structural changes (either in the organs of social control or in the adequacy of normative integration), or as spontaneous crowd reaction to the formation of publics and social movements.

2   The Other as Ideology

In his early writings[5], Marx (1978) develops his notions of alienation and emancipation. Whereas alienation refers to the loss of man's identity, emancipation denotes the possibility of recovering that identity through communist revolution. These notions presuppose two conditions: first, that man has a specific nature – one which could be lost; and second, that man is able to know this nature and recover it. Ideological alienation addresses the condition of domination which the subject experiences in capitalist society.

The term ideology connotes the presence of the other within the self: the thought of someone other than oneself dominates the thoughts/actions of the self. This 'co-habitation' of the other and the self produces peaceful relationships of domination, and the political dream of Marxism is to free the self entirely from the other. This is seen as a possible historical event, insofar as the other in Marx does not really exist; the other does not have a positive/real essence (as the self does), but is only the expression of an inverted consciousness or a state of alienation. "This State, this society, produces religion which is an inverted world consciousness, because they are an inverted world." (Marx, 1843/1978, p. 53.) True human nature (expressed in the notion of 'species being') can only flourish when the intruder/other has left the self.

Ideology, or 'conscience alienation', works on two different levels: one refers to the illusion of autonomy of consciousness (or religion alienation), and the other refers to class alienation, where the dominant class expresses its wishes and interests as the general wishes and interests of the whole society. According to Marx, human beings' forms of consciousness are determined by the material conditions of their lives. Thus, because of the division between material and mental labor, Marx follows, individuals engaged in mental labor think of themselves as unconditioned by material life-processes and as having a history and a power of their own. Furthermore, Marx stated that the production and diffusion of ideas are related to social

---

[5] Introduction to the *Contribution to the Critique of Hegel's Philosophy of Right* (1843), *The Jewish Question* (1843), *The German Ideology* (1845–46) and the *Economic and Philosophic Manuscripts* (1844), all published in *The Marx-Engels Reader*, edited by R. C. Tucker, 1978.

classes, since the ideas of the ruling classes are the ruling ideas of society. Ideology, in this sense, is a system of ideas which expresses the interest of the dominant class, but one which represents class relations only in an illusory form.

"And as society has hitherto moved in class antagonisms, morality has always been class morality; it has either justified the domination and the interests of the ruling class, or ever since the oppressed class became powerful enough, it has represented its indignation against this domination and the future interests of the oppressed." (Engels[6], 1878/1978, p. 726.) Since private property generates a separation of man from himself, from nature, and also from other men, its abolition is required to end human alienation.

To recover human nature is to recover its 'species-being' dimension: men will come out of themselves and their private interests and will live in a community of interests. Furthermore, emancipation will also entail the re-inversion of the inverted consciousness. This means that religion will no longer have an object. A new consciousness will be generated, a consciousness that will reflect the true nature of man.

Later Marxist theorists became more pessimistic about the possibility of emancipation: the other will never abandon the self because the self is already the other. A good example of this type of thinking is represented by the early Frankfurt School. Horkheimer and Adorno gave particular attention to the rise of the so-called 'culture industry' (Arato & E. Gebhardt, 1994; Horkheimer and Adorno, 1997), which describes the process of commodification of cultural forms brought about by the rise of the entertainment industries in Europe and the US in the late nineteenth and early twentieth centuries. These authors argued that the rise of the entertainment industries as capitalist enterprises resulted in the standardization and rationalization of cultural forms, and that this process atrophied the capacity of the individual to think and act in a critical and autonomous way. The cultural goods produced by the culture industry are designed and manufactured in accordance with the aims of capitalist accumulation and profit realization; they did not arise spontaneously from the masses themselves, but were tailored for consumption by the masses. In this process even art is considered as increasingly subsumed to the logic of commodity production and exchange and is seen as having lost the critical potential inherent in the very purposelessness of traditional artistic forms.

For Horkheimer and Adorno the development of the culture industry is intrinsic to the process of increasing rationalization and reification of modern societies, a process which renders individuals less capable of independent thinking and more de-

---

[6] Edited by Tucker (1987).

pendent on social processes over which they tend to have no control. Rather than providing a symbolic space within which individuals could cultivate their imagination, critical reflection and develop their individuality and autonomy, this commodified universe channels the energy of individuals into the collective consumption of standardized goods. "Real life is becoming indistinguishable from the movies. The sound film, far surpassing the theater of illusion, leaves no room for imagination or reflection on the part of the audience, who is unable to respond within the structure of the film, yet deviate from its precise detail without losing the thread of the story; hence the film forces its victims to equate it directly with reality." (Horkheimer and Adorno, 1997, p. 126.)

This last quote shows how, in this theory, the subject ends up being dominated by an alienating culture. There is no longer a source for difference between sameness and otherness. As has been expertly stated by H. Marcuse (1955), this process is possible because consumerist society is characterized by a match between the id (or the pleasure principle) and the super-ego (or the moral principle). What people ought to do is what gives them pleasure. There is no longer a source of dissonance between the individual and society, or between the self and the other.

3   Symbolic Interactionism: The Community of the Self and the Other

According to G. H. Mead, the self "is not initially there at birth but arises in the process of social experience and activity, that is, it develops in the given individual as a result of his relations to that process as a whole and to other individuals within that process" (Mead, 1977, p. 199). The self, therefore, arises in the process of learning, incorporating and actualizing the prevailing social codes that exist in society, and moreover, that this process of incorporation of social codes is what allows society itself to exist: "What makes society possible is such common responses, such organized attitudes, with reference to what we term property, the cults of religion, the process of education, and the relations of the family." (Mead, 1977, p. 225.)

This process Mead refers to as the incorporation of the 'generalized other', which means that the individual incorporates the attitudes of others towards itself and towards one another and this is expressed in the notion of 'me'. "The 'me' is the conventional, habitual individual. It is always there. It has to have those habits, those responses which everybody has; otherwise the individual could not be a member of the community." (Mead, 1967 p. 197.) What makes this process possible is the existence of a universal language which creates a universal community, where common symbols are utilized. However, the unique position of the self in its interactive process with society gives each individual a particular, unique standpoint which accounts for their individuality.

The second stage of the development of the full self corresponds not to the incorporation of social attitudes but to the active response of the self towards them. It takes place when the individual can direct his own behavior towards himself and towards others. In this moment of reflection and creative response different selves emerge; this is the moment of the 'I': "But an individual is always reacting to such an organized community in the way of expressing himself, not necessarily asserting himself in the offensive sense but expressing himself, being himself in such a co-operative process as belongs to any community." (Mead, 1967, p. 197.)

Since the instincts of cooperation and the feeling of interdependence are fundamental for the maintenance of society, Mead states that the individual is capable of changing the social structure according to the requirements of social evolution. Moreover, Mead states that the social ideal is the development of a perfected social intelligence, which would be the capacity of mutual understanding: "The development of communication is not simply a matter of abstract ideas, but is a process of putting one's self in the place of the other person's attitude, communicating through significant symbols." (Mead, 1977, p. 280.)

Social interaction, therefore, is a process that forms human conduct and it is not the mere expression or release of human conduct previously defined. This is because human beings, in order to act, take into account what the other is doing, and in doing so they modify their own conduct; to interact means to make indications to others on what to do, and also to interpret the indications made by others.

And who is the other in Mead's account? It is interesting to see that although Mead defines the other as constitutive of the self, there is no real other (as a radically different other) in this theory. According to Mead's view, the self and the other are tied together with their common symbols, which means that, potentially, symbols will allow them to have a perfected social intelligence. This perfected social setting that Mead describes, is the one that allows for both the expression of the self and the existence of social order.

4   Post-Structuralism and the Other as Power

Michel Foucault theorized modern power as self-surveillance (Foucault, 1978, 1979). The emergence of this new form of power is described as associated to the capitalist mode of economic organization where mass production required disciplined and productive workers. The new political system and the ideal of the sovereign state also required control of the freedom granted to the emergent individual: "The general juridical form that guaranteed a system of rights that were egalitarian in principle was supported by these tiny, everyday physical mechanisms, by all those systems of micro power that are essentially non egalitarian and asymmetrical that we call disciplines." (Foucault, 1979, p. 222.)

Therefore, changes in economy and politics made it necessary to train and educate the modern citizen, since, according to Foucault, the very objective of modern power is to assure order and efficiency of the human multiplicity.

This new power is characterized by the fact that it is not based on strong institutions – which work by controlling society downwards from the top – but is a kind of power which comes from below, which is exercised by the normalized individual himself. The previous figure of power, which was physically present, external, highly coercive and authoritative (represented in the body of the king), became something rather more abstract, yet more omnipresent and capable of taking control over even the microscopic and capillary human relationships. This new power corresponds to what Foucault calls disciplinary power, which is basically defined as the incorporation in each individual of the norms (or regimes of truth) of society, and the exercise of self-surveillance. The *panopticon* is the architectural figure of a prison which has the feature of producing a permanent state of conscious and permanent visibility that "assures an automatic functioning of power" (Foucault, 1979, p. 201).

Unlike the traditional conceptions of ideology, Foucault states that it is not possible to find a single responsible entity (such as a social class or institution, for example) in order to understand the normalization process, since it is a diffuse phenomenon that crosses society as a whole. Moreover, even though Foucault describes our society as following the same pattern of development (for instance in the assumption of sex as a taboo), he does not assume that there is a passive assimilation of the official norms of society. On the contrary, Foucault states that struggle and resistance are inherent in every power relationship. Far from being unidirectional and monolithic, power involves multiple confrontations and transformations, and there is no single issue that crosses the whole of society, but a multiplicity of them operating and competing at its basis. Law and state in this context are only the crystallization of a specific hegemonic strategy, which operates on the basis of other existing relations of power. Power is in no case allocated only to them.

The other in Foucault's theory of power is not language in general, but the type of oppressive discourse that disciplines the body and splits the subject. For Foucault –

even when he states that the subject is never fully disciplined, that normalization is never over – there is no space in the subject that resists normalization; no space that is not controlled by language. The possibility of autonomy in the subject will always depend on the external discursive offer: if the subject is normalized with oppressive discourse, he will have less freedom and spontaneity, and the contrary will happen if he is normalized with a liberating discourse. Resistance and struggle do not occur at the level at which a subject repels discourse (or resists the process of normalization), but at the level of (competing) discourses. His critique of power could be read as a claim for liberation, not from discourse in general, but from the particular discourse that disciplines the body, that makes it docile, that oppresses it. It is not a demand for the total abolition of power, but for the uncovering and transformation of existing power relations.

The other (as the presence of power) could eventually be eliminated.

5   Concluding Remarks: Desire as the Other?

Existing paradigms that explain violence depart from specific conceptions of the relation between the self and the other. As was argued at the beginning of this chapter, violence has so far been understood as an exceptional moment, in the same way that the presence of the other has been theorized as a temporary state of the self. None of these theories contemplate the possibility of the other, as an independent, radical or unreachable other.

The inclusion of the notion of desire as a constitutive aspect of the relation between the self and the other in current social and political theory seems to open up discussion in a new direction. However, as will become clear in what follows, this is possible only if desire is conceptualized as 'metonymic' (permanently changing its goal), and therefore never achieving satisfaction.

Since the publication of Axel Honneth's *The Struggle for Recognition* in 1996 the debate in political theory has experienced an important twist: purely proceduralist accounts of justice were no longer seen as sufficient accounts of democracy, since they did not consider major ethical questions, such as the nature of the ethical relation between the self and the other. The approach to this new dimension of the debate has been inspired by the dialectic of recognition presented by Hegel in the *Phenomenology of the Spirit*. What is interesting, however, is that this twist, which meant a return to ethics (Garber, 2000), did not seriously take into account what in Kojeve's view was the most important aspect of the Hegelian shift, which was to acknowledge not only the presence of the other but the presence of the *desire of the desire of the other*. He left out of his analysis the power relations involved in the possibilities of recognition and he did not include the problematic relation of jealously that desire entails. Taking a purely normative stand, he simply concluded that in given objective and subjective conditions the self and the other will be able not only to communicate and live peacefully next to other, but that the self and the other could realize themselves through mutual recognition: their mutual desires of the desire of the other would be then satisfied (very similar to Mead's understanding of perfected social intelligence). "Put positively, this means that the history of human spirit is to be understood as a conflictual process in which the 'moral' potential inherent in natural ethical life (as something 'enclosed' and not yet unfolded) is gradually generalized." (Honneth, 1996, p. 15.) Honneth thus fully embraces the already deflated ideas of modernism and progress.

Honneth's *Struggle for Recognition* simply adds to the list of social theorists who see that otherness and difference can be ultimately reduced to the sameness of the self: the boundary of the self and the other, either through rational agreement, through symbolic empathy, or through discursive construction, would eventually disappear.

Now, one has to ask whether violence can be equated to lack of recognition. My short answer is no. Violence cannot be understood only in this *negative* way – as a 'lack'. On the contrary, the very nature of violence is that it is productive. Violence is always accompanied by the generation of a particular meaning and desire about the enemy. It is precisely here that the misconception of the notions of otherness and desire become central: contrary to what Honneth claims, the relationship with the other is permanently marked by an interruption or impossibility. The desire of the desire of the other not only opens the door for recognition (as a demand for love), but also leads to a relationship of aggressive jealousy *(your joy is my misery)* and hate.

In the following chapter I will present a new paradigm to understand violence, incorporating desire as the barrier that prevents the full inclusion of the other within the self.

Chapter 2: On Sacredness and Transgression: Understanding Social Antagonism

This chapter explores the nature of violence. In particular, and mostly through the reading of Durkheim (1965, 1984), Schmitt (1994, 1996), and Lacan (1977, 1978), I argue that social antagonism and its violent expression cannot be understood if social theory does not conceptualize radical otherness as the pre-condition of society. Moreover, I argue that only by adding the category of enjoyment (pleasure derived from transgression), can we begin to grasp what collective violence – at least in modern societies – is about. Though they had different arguments and purposes, these authors were capable of not only seeing the negative (the excluded) element within every social identity, but also the foundational character of it (exclusion as a precondition for the identity to exist). Although much of current social and political theory is preoccupied with the other in general, this other is one that accounts for difference and calls for recognition. In contrast to those accounts, this paper explores how a 'radical other' – with whom there is a relation of antagonism – is constituted.

I start my argument with a critique of radical contingency and by addressing the presence of a *sacred* boundary in each identity. The sacred, expressed in a transcendental narrative about society, attempts, but fails to (entirely) conceal the precarious character of society. That is, though society self-institutes itself and denies its contingency for the sake of its stability, it is never able to erase its experience of vulnerability.

Framed this way, social antagonism is the act of excluding a certain other from social life, who, as the result of the mechanism of projection, appears as the cause of the vulnerability of society. Though 'othering' is a permanent social process, social exclusion can be accompanied by different degrees of hostility and violence.[7]

In the second section of the chapter, I claim that social antagonism is existential. The Schmittean notions of the *enemy* and of the *political*, illustrate that social antagonism does not express a conflict within the symbolic universe (i.e. differences of power, or interpretation), but it expresses a conflict between the symbolic and non-symbolic ones. The enemy embodies a threat to the very existence of the self.

---

[7] The excluded other is usually defined by his/her ascribed status (such as nationality, race, ethnicity, gender), though often acquired ones (sexual orientation and political beliefs) define exclusion.

In order to understand the physicality of violence[8], in the third and fourth part of the chapter, I present the psychoanalytical notions of the *unconscious* and of *fantasy*, respectively. The subject of the unconscious is a 'castrated' subject who has given up enjoyment (the mother) to enter the world of language. Once again, the lack of enjoyment that the subject experiences is projected into the excluded other, who appears (this time) as stealing enjoyment from the self. The relation of antagonism between the self and the other, then, is not only existential but libidinal and is characterized by aggressive jealousy; only the destruction (or suffering) of the other seems to satisfy the self.

As we can see, social antagonism and violence are ambivalent in nature. Ethical claims (usually about the restoration of the symbolic-moral order) go hand in hand with what appears to be a clear denial of that very same symbolic order (enjoyment of the exclusion of the other). Religious extremism (or openly religiously motivated forms of violence) shows this logic in its purest expression. The lack of any religious affiliation in secular perpetrators of violence, however, should not lead us to ignore the *religious character* of collective violence. The best examples are found in torture, where prisoners are subjected to extreme physical and psychological pain, because they represent a 'moral threat' to the wellbeing of society.[9] The ethical claim that justifies violence appears as a moral duty (or as a 'calling', to use Weber's term) to act against a perceived threat to the existence of the social.[10] This relation of antagonism between the self and the other might be expressed in different forms of collective violence (state violence, hate crime, political violence, etc.), depending on who defines the other as a threat to society, who attempts to 'save' society from that threat, and how they attempt to go about it.

1   The Sacred and the Profane

The question of the possibility of the social has occupied a central place in sociology from its earliest times. Durkheim's insights in *The Division of Labor* (1984), and more radically in *The Elementary Forms of Religious Life* (1965), somehow anticipated the kind of answer we are trying to find here. For Durkheim the possibility of

---

[8] This usually remains unexplained by sociology. The most paradigmatic cases are strategic accounts of collective violence. See Charles Tilly, 1978.

[9] Even when violence accompanies social transformation, there is a discourse of 'restoration' of what has been lost, i.e. 'humanity'.

[10] See Vidal's (2000) study on torture in Chile.

the social lay in the existence of a collective consciousness, or collective representation, which would establish a moral bond within a community. Contrary to contractualist theories of society, which hold that already constituted individualities meet according to their necessities, Durkheim stated that for such exchange between individuals to exist, another force must have been operating prior to the exchange, a force that would guarantee the stability of such exchange. This earlier social force he defined as 'pre-contractual' solidarity, which consisted of the shared feeling of sameness, belonging and obligation. These feelings are, according to Durkheim, the result of the religious experience that accompanies social life: "In a general way, it is unquestionable that a society has all that is necessary to arouse the Sensation of the divine in minds, merely by the power that it has over them; (...). It requires that, forgetful of our own interest, we make ourselves its servitors, and it submits us to every sort of inconvenience, privation and sacrifice, without which social life would be impossible. (...). It is this ascendancy that we call moral authority." (Durkheim, 1984, p. 206.)

Religion, Durkheim states, is characterized by the classification of all things into two domains: the sacred and the profane. "Sacred things are those which the interdictions protect and isolate; profane things, those to which these interdictions are applied and which must remain at a distance from the first." (Durkheim, 1965, p. 56.) Religious beliefs, on the other hand, are "the representations which express the nature of sacred things and the relations which they sustain, either with each other or with profane things", and rites "are the rules of conduct which prescribe how a man should comport himself in the presence of these sacred objects" (Durkheim, 1965, p. 56).

Though in pre-modern societies it is easier to see the function of the sacred, Durkheim argues, modern societies still rely on the collective consciousness that results from the very interdependence that division of labor produces for their existence. Indeed, the whole argument in *The Division of Labor* is that difference can only sustain itself as a form of solidarity, based on the homogeneity it produces.

Durkheim saw the instability of the social bond and the permanent *anomic* threat to it and so could also see the conditions under which such a moral bond could exist and be reproduced in modern societies. It is well known that for Durkheim religion is not only a system of beliefs, but a system of practices pertaining to sacred things: "The collective ideas and sentiments are even possible only owing to these exterior movements which symbolize them, as we have established. Then it is action, which dominates the religious life, because of the mere fact that it is society which is its source." (Durkheim, 1965, p. 466.)

There are several remarkable aspects about this theory. Firstly, Durkheim sees society as the result of a feeling, rather than a rational agreement between individuals. Secondly, this feeling confers a sacred character on such bonds, which, as we have seen, accounts for the origin of religion itself; still more interesting, it is the consequence of this character. The status of the sacred in this theory does not account for the psychological quest for meaning – or for salvation as in Weber's (1958) theory of religion – but actually implies the foundational moment of society or its ontological possibility. Societies, according to Durkheim, are always religious in this sense, that is, religion cannot be entirely isolated from the phenomenon of society as sacred. Contrary to inter-subjectivist accounts of subjectivity, Durkheim understood individuality and differences, though of course existent, as marked or framed within a foundational moment, and certainly not as the point of departure for the process of the formation of society.

Having assigned a constitutive role to the moral bond (or religion), Durkheim (1984) naturally saw in the process of modernization and secularization the risks that losing such bonds would entail for the stability of the social. However, because of the necessary (foundational) character of sacredness for the existence of society, this radical aspect of reality cannot just disappear. On the contrary, it has to survive and somehow accommodate itself to the different processes and challenges that modernization presents to social cohesion. It could therefore be argued that the character of the sacred as a foundational moment, though sometimes secularized, has the same function that it has in its purely religious version. Contemporary studies (Dayan and Katz, 1992) have indeed shown how the development of mass media has contributed to the existence of mass ceremonies, which, like the rituals in Durkheim's theory of religion, reinforce existing social bonds in so-called 'media events'. From this perspective, even collective violence could be considered as a ceremony, or as a sacrifice, since it is clearly a moment where social cohesion, among the aggressors and also among the oppressed, is achieved.

2   Emergence of Social Antagonism

In order to summarize the argument made so far, we can use Castoriadis's (1996, 1998) interpretation: society self-institutes itself but denies its own invention for the sake of its stability. Denying its contingent character, society creates a transcendent narrative about its own origin but since this narrative fails to conceal the existence of a prior pre-symbolic and meaningless pure being, society keeps experiencing a threat which this abyss presents to the constitution of society. It is interesting to note how Durkheim (1965, 1984) could see this radical moment of the constitution of the social, but he was not able to measure its entire dynamic, which consists of the social antagonism that can emerge from the omnipotent *fear* of absolute disintegration; the world outside social solidarity is not the realm of the different, but of the un-nameable (that which is not, or cannot be, incorporated into the symbolic universe). I would argue that it has not been the actual lack of social bonds (anomie) that has caused the major violent outbursts in history, but the fear of the loss of such a bond, which guarantees the social. In a purely anomic situation, social disintegration prevails, there are no sources for homogeneity, and there is a state of pure dislocation. Moreover, in anomie there is such multiplicity of otherness that finally the logic of exclusion, as the precondition for the constitution of the social and of social antagonism, disappears.

Social antagonism refers not to the conflict within the symbolic sphere, but to the expression of the conflict between the symbolic and non-symbolic ones. This is why violence does not necessarily occur when there is a loss of sense of meaning (or disenchantment), nor when there is a difference of interpretation about that meaning, nor when there is an irreconcilable difference of interests between the parties. Instead of violence, lack of meaning is likely to produce individual withdrawal from society (Weber, 1978). Different interpretations are likely to lead to the emergence of discursive spaces in which attempts are made to find some understanding or means of persuasion (Habermas, 1962). Different interests will somehow resolve issues through bargaining, compromise and some sort of domination according to the power held by the parties (Marx, 1978).

Social antagonism, contrary to social disorganization and episodic violence, is the act of exclusion of those who are considered to threaten the fragile/contingent symbolic integrity of society. Naked violence emerges when identity itself is threatened; when what is feared is the total loss of the symbolic titles that cover the prior – the *asocial* state of pure dislocation or anomie. As Castoriadis puts it: "Hobbes was right, though for the wrong reasons. Fear of death is indeed the mainstay of institutions. Not the fear of being killed by the next man but the justified fear that everything, even meaning, will dissolve." (Castoriadis, 1998, p. 136.)

Carl Schmitt's (1994, 1996) critique of liberalism shares some of the premises presented here. The most obvious one is his awareness of the ever-present possibility of antagonism and the violence that might result from it. Most interesting, however, is his critique of individual reductionism (or what he refers to as a theory of pluralism) and his references instead to something bigger than individuals' single rationalities and associations (a 'social fact' in Durkheim's language). To express this idea he recalls Sorel's myth of the general strike, which was able to mobilize workers, not out of reason or pragmatism, but out of the depths of a genuine life instinct. Out of this experience, Schmitt continues, "springs the great enthusiasm, the great moral decision and the great myth" (Schmitt, 1994, p. 68). Schmitt argues, as I will here, that antagonism results not from moral, economic or aesthetic interpretations, but from the existential sphere (and therefore exceeds rationality). "If such physical destruction of human life is not motivated by an existential threat to one's own way of life, then it cannot be justified, in the same way as war cannot be justified by ethical and juristic norms. If there really are enemies in the existential sense as meant here, then it is justified, but only politically, to repel and fight them physically." (Schmitt, 1996, p. 49.) The political, according to Carl Schmitt, is the particular differentiation between friends and enemies, and as such he defines it as the most intense and extreme form of antagonism. Schmitt argues that the state is the decisive political entity and, accordingly, he proposes to attribute to it the power to declare war on the enemy as a way of ensuring its own survival. "War is the existential negation of the enemy." (Schmitt, 1996, p. 33.)

Though Schmitt centers his analysis on the state and on the possibility (even necessity) of declaring war against another nation, analytically he does not reduce the possibility of friend-enemy groupings to that level alone. Indeed, he openly mentions the possibility of internal conflicts within a nation, which may lead to civil war. What he stresses, though, is that such antagonism will be the effect of the politicization of other fields of social life where the friend-enemy grouping has emerged.

Following Schmitt's argument one could go further and state that every social identity has the potential to become political and as such might enter into an antagonistic relation with a certain enemy. Indeed, I would argue that whenever there is a moral discourse accompanying collective violence, some sort of social antagonism is at play. On the other hand, poorly constituted hegemonies, in which sacred elements of the past no longer fulfill the same cohesive function as in the present, give rise to hybrid forms of social antagonism; a mixture of random (anomic) violence takes place together with collective (antagonistic) violence.

Weber (1958) theorized the sacred in a different way. For him, the sacred refers to the quest for salvation: the question about the divine and the answer that organizes and gives meaning to the life of a people. Usually, Weber and Durkheim are presented as thinkers that inaugurated different schools and sociological traditions but reading Weber's account of religion from the perspective presented here, one could also argue that the experience of suffering itself is the result of the open 'dualism' (of chaos and meaning or anomie and social solidarity) and of the impossibility of eradicating the non-symbolic threat definitively. Durkheim's and Weber's accounts of religion would not contradict each other, but would account for different moments in the formation and stabilization of society.

I would like to stress the difference between the sacred as foundational and the sacred as the quest for meaning. The sacred as foundational expresses the original definition of the boundaries of the social, where the spaces for possible and prohibited actions are defined. This leads to Freud's (1950) analysis of the relation between totemic religions (the first known forms of organized religion) and the existence of taboos (which account for the prohibition of incest). The distinction between these two types of sacredness is fundamental for our purposes here. Durkheim allows us to see the radicalism of the social as the act excluding the non-social, and Weber allows us to see the different ways in which different cultures address this dualism. Actually, Weber's (1958) typology of types of religious rationality (which I will also refer in next chapter) comes in very handy when trying to understand the phenomenon of violence: the ascetic would actively intervene within the world and try to eliminate the dualism (or the origin of the suffering); the mystic would sublimate the conflict and try to find a personal and inner solution to it (and would therefore not transform the world or the possible causes of suffering); the dualistic (found in Zoroastrianism) would acknowledge the presence of two principles, good and evil.

The theoretical premise about the foundational act of violence and exclusion on which every society is built acquires specificity and historicity only when a theoretical tool – such as Weber's typology – is incorporated into the analysis. Otherwise, only an inexorable gap divides the existential claim and the reality of concrete societies. In light of Weber's theory of religion, one could argue that the various expressions of violence against otherness (and the way each of these societies addresses those violent outbursts) are related to the way the sacred boundary of each society has been constructed.

3 Language and the Structure of Desire

The relation of antagonism presents yet another dimension, this time related to the enjoyment that the exclusion of the other produces in the self. Indeed, the child is separated from the mother as well as protected from the mother's desire. "The fundamental fantasy – or habitual way of seeing and relating to the world – can be viewed as a response to separation." (Fink, 2000, p. 57.)

Lacan's most important contribution to psychoanalysis is precisely his conceptual-ization of the unconscious and the metonymic character of desire. Contrary to the self-aware and transparent subject of the Cartesian *cogito*, the positive dialogical subject of symbolic interactionism and the normalizing subject of functionalism and post-structuralism, the Lacanian subject incorporates its own impossibility within it-self. Beyond language, beyond the social, is the 'real', pure pulsing drive and by-product of an incomplete process of symbolization. By focusing on this failure of symbolization, Lacan is able to define the unconscious as a radical other, which is not linguistified through any process of communication and therefore allows no emancipatory psycho-analytical therapy.

Since the unconscious emerges at the entrance of the symbolic order, Lacan theo-rizes it by considering the nature not only of the subject, but also the nature of lan-guage. Following Saussure (1959), Lacan tells us that the sign is different from the symbol: the symbol represents something for somebody, it maintains a certain conti-nuity between what is being represented and the means of representation; the sign, on the other hand, is arbitrary. The sign is composed of the signifier (which corre-sponds to the acoustic image) and the signified (the concept). The signifier is au-tonomous, self-governing and independent; it has a colonizing power over the signi-fied. In this framework, words acquire meaning not in relation to the objects that they represent but according to their position in the signifying chain.

This definition of language has enormous consequences for both the formation of subjectivity and the possibility of inter-subjectivity (full recognition). Language will always be 'the other' as different and separated from the 'sameness' of the subject. Language, as a wall, does not allow the subject to find its own being, to find its *truth*. Though the subject emerges in the field of the other (of language) and owes its own existence as man to the other, the being of the subject is different from language, and cannot wholly be expressed by it. There is something beyond language that consti-tutes the space of lack in the subject, a part of it cannot find representation, and this is the condition of the subject's desire. "Desire is neither the appetite for satis-faction, nor the demand for love, but the difference that results from the subtraction of the first from the second, their phenomenon of their splitting … ." (Lacan, 1977, p. 287.)

The subject is defined as 'lacking' in the sense that it depends on the signifier, and this signifier is, as Lacan states, primarily in the field of the other. The subject will always be in a state of alienation because of this structure of language and its relation to the subject. Not only because the source of satisfaction continues to be situated outside the self (imaginary identification with external images), but also because the subject sees its own desire as the other's desire. Lacan states that it seems as if the subject could eventually choose between being represented by language (and being part of the world of meaning) *or* simply being. This 'or', however, demonstrates the essential alienation of the subject, for if it chooses meaning, being is left out, and if it chooses being, there is no way of saying so. "If we choose being, the subject disappears, it eludes us, it falls into non-meaning. If we choose meaning, the meaning survives only deprived of the part of non-meaning, that is (…) that which constitutes in the realization of the subject, the unconscious." (Lacan, 1978, p. 211.)

Desire, strictly speaking, has no object. Once the subject gets what it wants, desire vanishes. Fink (2000) states that hysteria and obsession are simply two different modes of keeping desire alive. The hysterical person will make sure he/she remains dissatisfied with what he/she gets, the obsessive does the same by wanting the unattainable. Lacan calls the cause of desire *object a*, which is by nature metonymic (it will keep changing as a way of keeping desire alive).

4 Fantasy

The stated features of language, desire and subjectivity, are expressed inter-subjectively in the impossibility of full recognition and in the relation of aggressive jealousy between the self and the other. There is always a blank space, a margin of doubt, about the other's desire: *"You are telling me this, but what do you really want?"* This uncertainty about what the other really wants leads us to fantasy.

Fantasy functions as a construction, as an overproduction of meaning. It is an imaginary scenario filling out the void, the opening of *the desire of the other*. "By giving us an answer to the question 'what does the other want?', it enables us to evade the unbearable deadlock in which the other wants something from us, but we are at the same time incapable of translating this desire of the other into a positive interpellation, into a mandate with which to identify." (Zizek, 1997, p. 114.) Fantasy plays the role of concealing this inconsistency. It gives a framework through which we experience the world as consistent and meaningful.

The nature of this narrative is still more complex than it appears at first sight. The transcendental narrative not only establishes the law, it also frames desire: "what the law prohibits, (unconscious) desire seeks" (Fink, 2000, p. 207). Fantasy not only gives a sense of wholeness to the identity, but it also involves enjoyment whilst transgressing, so the 'expressed' discourse about the excluded other is always accompanied by a hidden experience of enjoyment of othering and excluding.

The other, according to this theory, not only threatens the possibility of meaning, but moreover the possibility of enjoyment. The excluded other is guilty of preventing the self from fulfilling its desire, of stealing the self's enjoyment. The self-other relation then, is one of aggressive jealousy. The self cannot satisfy its desire, because the other is 'enjoying too much'. Let me clarify this point by quoting Zizek: "What bothers us in the other (Jew, Japanese, African, Turk…) is that he appears to entertain a privileged relationship to the object – the other either possesses the object treasure, having snatched it away from us (which is why we don't have it) or poses a threat to our possession of the object. In short, the skinhead's intolerance of the other cannot be adequately conceived without a reference to the object-cause of desire that is, by definition, missing." (Zizek, 1994, p. 71.)

Thus what characterizes aggressive jealousy is that, on the one hand, the subject feels deprived of something which he considers his due and which has been taken away by his rival, and, on the other, that he not only "sickens at the sight of enjoyment (…) but he is easy only at the misery of others" (Klein, 1975, p. 181).

As Zizek states, fantasy is the necessary counterpart of the real: "Fantasy conceals the fact that the other, the symbolic order, is structured around some traumatic impossibility, around something, which cannot be symbolized – i.e. the real of *jouissance*: through fantasy, *jouissance* is domesticated, gentrified … ." (Zizek, 1997, p. 123.) As such, fantasy frames our desire (our own space of failed interpellation). It teaches us *how to desire*, and because of the metonymic structure of desire, the excluded other remains a "spectral object which does not have positive ontological consistency but that fills the gap of the constitutive impossibility" (Zizek, 1997, p. 76).

5   Discussion and Conclusions

The purpose of this chapter was to show the inescapable presence of otherness and exclusion, and the relation between violence and enjoyment. Using Durkheim's terminology rather loosely, I said that anomie corresponds to the primordial asocial state of lack of meaning (the universe of pure drives), social solidarity corresponds to the relationship that emerges between those who are united by the same moral bond (the symbolic universe); whereas social antagonism corresponds to the overproduction of meaning (or fantasy) about the excluded other and the enjoyment of its exclusion. Since anomie has been prohibited (repressed) from the very beginning of the existence of society, fantasy is not about anomie itself, but about what seems to threaten the stability of such repression. Furthermore, social solidarity and social antagonism are sacred insofar as they are *sine qua non* conditions for the existence of the social. Solidarity establishes exclusion (it defines what is prohibited) and thereby makes society possible. Antagonism breaks the established symbolic universe (it does what is prohibited) and thereby protects the stability of the social identity. Because social antagonism involves a transgression of the moral order, at least part of its real content remains a secret among those who have joyfully transgressed the law.

Violence, seen from this perspective, is the 'acting out' of the fantasy about the other. It is a ceremony enacted to strengthen the weakened social bond.

There are at least two questions that arise from this chapter. First: does this framework allow the understanding of cultural and historical variations regarding social antagonism and violence? And second: is it possible to include the notion of recognition in the model?

To answer these questions fairly a more complex argument is required, since new concepts need to be added to make those theoretical articulations possible. However, with this caveat in mind, I would like to offer some preliminary observations.

One way of answering the first question is to think of a set of feminine ethics that could transcend our patriarchal social organization. I will develop this argument at length in the next chapter but for now I will present a brief summary of the main ideas.

Whilst there is, by definition, a sacred boundary around every identity, the construction of the excluded other is variable since *different identities have different relations to what they exclude*.

One way of understanding this is using Lacan's theory of sexual difference where transgression, or *phallic jouissance*, and *feminine jouissance* represent different modes of experiencing enjoyment (masculine and feminine respectively) and thus are *the* differentiating criteria for the emergence (or absence) of social antagonism. The incorporation of sexuality into the analysis of violence would allow us to state that the ethical claims of the restoration of the social order as well as the enjoyment of the other's exclusion are not gender neutral, but that they are male ethical claims and male forms of enjoyment. In our patriarchal society particular types of gender and sexual identities are fostered, and those identities are framed by a primarily masculine (or Oedipal) super-ego (morality). Masculinity and femininity have defined their sacred boundaries in different ways, and therefore relate to what they exclude differently too. Male identity is entirely caught up in the symbolic order (because of the nature of male castration) and therefore male enjoyment consists of transgressing the symbolic order to reach the realm of the drives. Feminine identity, in contrast, is not only in the symbolic order, but also connected to what is outside of it (the real). *Feminine jouissance*, then, is a way of enjoying that does not need to break free from the symbolic order or transgress it. Since what lies outside the realm of the symbolic is what threatens the identity and produces social antagonism, the more 'feminine' and less patriarchal the society, the less the experience and fear of social disintegration. Also, the more feminine the society, the smaller the need is to transgress the symbolic order to enjoy.

The second question was about the possibility of recognition. Though the argument presented here states that even in a democracy there is exclusion and that recognition is never able to entirely erase fantasy, I want to underscore the importance of political and cultural openness. In fact, fantasy, as the arbitrary construction of the other and the enjoyment of its exclusion, and recognition, as the possibility of mutual understanding, are directly related. That is to say, the increase of one is always at the expense of the other. As I mentioned above, fantasy requires the excluded other to remain a 'spectral object' without any positive ontological consistency. From this statement it follows that the presence of discursive spaces, where the definitions of identity and of the other are deconstructed and compared, are indeed crucial, since by destabilizing fixed fantasies they prevent the emergence of social antagonism. Though there will always be a negation of a certain degree of the other, its survival would grant it the possibility of its later inclusion in the community. I hope the normative disagreement with Schmitt has become clear. Whereas he claims the need to assign to the state the necessary power to define the enemy and act against it, I claim the need to continually deconstruct the constitutive outsider in order to prevent it from reaching the status of real enemy. Although politically this statement appears simple enough, at a theoretical level the construction of a bridge between fantasy and recognition requires the tracing of the central concept at stake: the Hegelian *desire of the desire of the other*.

Chapter 3: Sexuality and Violence: Towards Feminine Ethics

The general aim of this chapter is to show that collective violence not only seeks the restoration of a social order, but the restoration – or reinforcement – of a *masculine law* or patriarchal social order. Such a social order entails a particular mode of enjoyment *(phallic jouissance)*, as a specific form of transgressing the law.[11] Thus, violence and exclusion will be regarded here as expressions of a masculine form of enjoying transgression of the symbolic order, and paradoxically, as ways of restoring such an order. In this framework the excluded other, *par excellence*, is *feminine desire*, associated in our masculine culture with passivity and disintegration.

1 The Key Nature of Sexuality

As will be shown in what follows, sexuality will be the key notion around which identity formation and exclusion will be theorized. Sexuality, however, will not be simplified to mean any biological difference, but will be understood as different ways of 'enjoying'. To put it differently, sexuality will account for the different positions that the subject (men and women) can take regarding the object of desire and the law (or language). Let me clarify this point. There are at least two ways of asserting such a claim: the first is the hardline Freudian/Lacanian perspective, which states that men and women are *per se*, 'structurally' different; whilst the second introduces a qualification: men and women are indeed structurally different *in the context* of an existing patriarchal society. I will adopt the second perspective and claim that *there is a particular sexual structure that presents itself in a particular social context*, by which I mean that in our society femininity and masculinity are *framed* by a primarily masculine morality. This is based on the understanding that the symbiotic relationship that exists between the mother and child (described as 'passive') can only be broken by a third ('active') element, which according to Freud, is the role of the father (and in Lacan the symbolic *Name of the Father* or paternal metaphor).

---

[11] According to Slavoj Zizek, every social order is based not only on certain law, but also on a certain way of transgressing such law.

According to these theories, the undifferentiated pre-social is the first experience that needs to be repressed for meaning to arise. The emergence of meaning and differentiation requires activity, which, according to Freud can *only* be provided by the father. Feminine passivity is repressed and it is masculine activity instead which allows the child to become autonomous and gendered. According to Lacan, on the other hand, both girls and boys only have one 'signifier' – that of masculine desire (or the signifier of the phallus) – which they both draw on in becoming women and men. The repression of passivity and the lack of a signifier for feminine desire are the starting point for a critique of exclusion and violence.

At this very preliminary stage we are already confronted with the question of whether *the feminine* is as passive as it is portrayed in Freud's theory. The short answer to this question is no. Femininity, from a Lacanian perspective, involves action. Women go through repression as men do, except that this repression is different and this difference accounts for non-radical action/repression (women are not entirely bound by the symbolic). The feminine position, though incorporated into the world of language, still remains connected to the world of being (or the real), which the masculine identity entirely represses. The relation of femininity to what is excluded is therefore not as radical as the masculine relation to it. Although there is enough action for feminine subjectivity to emerge, it nonetheless allows for some sort of recognition of what has been repressed in order to allow that action/individuality to emerge. As will be seen in what follows, this non-radical action shows us an interesting mode of dealing with otherness and exclusion. Lacan (1998) links this feminine position to sublimation and mysticism.

Other question also arise: is it possible not to repress passivity and feminine desire at all? What is the role of feminine desire in our society? Is it possible to have a fair division of labor between masculine and feminine desire? What types of societies are fostered out of possible nomenclatures between these types of desire? Is it possible to transcend the Oedipus complex/masculine morality? Some of these questions will be addressed in what follows. Certainly they have already been addressed by feminist psychoanalysts,[12] who, from positions closer to or further from either Freud or Lacan, have provided critical theory with new elements that enable us to reconsider our society.

Max Weber's studies on world religions can also shed light on this discussion. According to him, Judeo-Christian, Oriental Hinduism, Buddhism and Zoroastrian religious traditions express different ways of dealing with suffering and conferring

---

[12] The works of Jessica Benjamin (1995) and Joan Copjec (2003) are particularly interesting.

meaning on action. Though all of them can be said to be active (since they all favor primal repression of the profane), their activity and their manner of dealing with what they repress is indeed different. While the first one (the Judeo-Christian tradition) actively intervenes in the world in God's name, the second (oriental Buddhism and Hinduism) directs this action inwards and, through contemplation, attempts to possess the sacred. Zoroastrianism, on the other hand, is a 'dualistic' religion in which action and passivity are combined and the presence of two principles of life, good and evil, is accepted.

2 A Masculine Society: The Oedipus Complex and Morality

From a Freudian/Lacanian perspective, two things are indisputable: subjects are *sexed subjects* and society can only be *patriarchal*. Let us begin with the patriarchal society. The basic idea here is that the father (or the death of the father in Freud) enables meaning, autonomy and morality to exist.

In *Group Psychology and the Analysis of the Ego*, Freud (1959) states that the earliest emotional tie between a person and another person consists of identification: "Identification is known to psychoanalysis as the earliest expression of an emotional tie with another person. It plays a part in the early history of the Oedipus complex. A little boy will exhibit a special interest in his father; he would like to grow like him and be like him, and take his place everywhere. We may say simply that his father is his ideal." (Freud, 1959, p. 46.)

At the same time however, the child develops a true sexual object-cathexis with his mother. These two ties subsist side by side until the Oedipus complex takes place. The boy realizes that the father stands between his mother and himself, therefore his identification with his father grows hostile, and he wishes he could entirely replace the father. The standard resolution of this complex entails the child giving up his mother and over-identifying with his father, thus the boy acquires his masculine character. The complementary process occurs for the girl, who ends up giving up her father, over-identifying with her mother, and acquiring a feminine character. Masculinity and femininity, as Freud understood them, correspond to activity and passivity respectively. According to Elizabeth Grosz (1990), the (active) boy makes a pact with the father: he gives up his mother in exchange for the promise of deferred satisfaction with a woman of his own. This pact would found patriarchy anew in each generation: "guaranteeing the son's position as heir to the father's position in so far as he takes on the father's attributes. In exchange for sacrificing his relation to the mother, whom he now recognizes as 'castrated', the boy identifies with the authority invested in the father" (Grosz, 1990, p. 68). For the girl, things are different. For her, the Oedipus complex brings no rewards, no authority or compensation for her abandonment of her mother: "It rather entails the acceptance of subordination." (Grosz, 1990, p. 69.)

In *The Ego and the Id* Freud (1960) develops the element that allows this process to take place and be resolved at length: the *super-ego* or *moral agency* of the subject. The super-ego, in Freud's theory, is what allows desire for the mother to be repressed, the repression of hate for the father, and subsequent over-identification with the father to take place. Indeed, according to Freud, the differentiation of the super-ego from the ego is one of the most important characteristics of the development of both the individual and the species: "The super-ego is, however, not simply a residue of the earliest object-choices of the id; it also represents an energetic reaction-formation against those choices. Its relation to the ego is not exhausted by the precept: 'you ought to be like this (like your father)'. It also comprises the prohibition: 'you may not do all that he does; some things are his prerogative.' This double aspect of the ego ideal derives from the fact that the ego ideal had the task of repressing the Oedipus complex." (Freud, 1960, p. 30.) According to Freud, the super-ego retains the character of the father, and he further states: "the more powerful the Oedipus complex was and the more rapidly it succumbed to repression (under the influence of authority, religious teaching, schooling and reading), the stricter will be the domination of the super-ego over the ego later on – in the form of conscience or perhaps of an unconscious sense of guilt" (Ibid, p. 31). As we can see, the super-ego is entirely paradoxical. On the one hand, it makes it imperative for the son to be like his father and yet he cannot really be like the father since he cannot have his mother. On the other hand, the more the super-ego is obeyed, the stronger the feeling of guilt.

Freud goes even further and states that the presence of the super-ego may indeed account for the origin of religion: "The self-judgment which declares that the ego falls short of its ideal produces the religious sense of humility to which the believer appeals in his longing." (Ibid, p. 33.) In other words, the presence in men of a strong super-ego humiliates them. This argument is developed at length in *Totem and Taboo* (Freud, 1950).[13]

In Lacanian psychoanalysis the function of the father is similar, although Lacan analyses sexual drives always through the functioning of language and linguistic

---

[13] In *Totem and Taboo*, Freud explores the causes of the taboo of incest and of killing on the basis of a primal horde composed by a band of brothers who had killed their father.

processes. The paternal metaphor is what separates the child from the mother, and thereby grants the child access to the world of language. The *father* (not the real father but the symbolic father) is the one who represents the fundamental structure of the symbolic order: "... the father's name was that which had to be invoked in order to maintain the incest taboo and which sent forbidden desires, in disguise, on their circuitous journeys through language" (Bowie, 1991, p. 13). The father can play this role of ultimate authority since his relation of paternity is more a symbolic paternity than a biological one: the father is a *name* because ultimately paternity always involves something beyond the biological reality. The metaphor of the *Name of the Father* expresses how the law – the primordial prohibition belonging to the order of the symbolic (to the order of culture and not to the order of nature) – imposes itself upon man.

Lacan (1977) links this space of lack of the subject, and his desire that can never be satisfied, to the castration complex. According to him, the phallus is the main signifier, and as such belongs to the realm of the other. The phallus of the father (the symbolic father) is what inaugurates the child's access to the symbolic order. Moreover, the *Name of the Father* – as the prohibition of incest – is the constitutive principle of the symbolic order. The phallus in this sense is the first or main signifier, and as such, is the one that breaks the imaginary relation between the mother and the child. However, since it is a signifier, nobody can ever possess it: "The fact that the phallus is a signifier means that it is in the place of the other that the subject has access to it." (Lacan, 1977, p. 288.)

Since the phallus remains in the domain of the other, the subject constantly suffers from its absence – and therefore experiences the castration complex.[14]

3 Feminine Passivity versus Male Activity

That said, the question still remains as to why it is the father – rather than the mother – who inaugurates the child's entry into the symbolic order?

According to Freud and Lacan, initially the child sees its mother as a phallic mother. The first relation of the child with the mother is just a continuation of the previous symbiotic uterine relationship. Later on, the child realizes that the mother 'has a lack'. Freud would reduce this to awareness of the lack of a penis. Lacan translates

---

[14] The object petit *a* could work as a substitution for the phallus. It is the object of desire used by the subject in order to avoid the castration complex and allows an immediate relation of enjoyment without mediation of the symbolic order.

this as awareness of a lack in the mother. She is no longer perceived to be omnipotent. At this stage Freud formulates the first differentiation between activity and passivity. The child in this pre-Oedipal stage finds itself in a passive position regarding
its mother and this passivity involves a sort of reaction and active repetition. It also
entails a certain enjoyment of the mother-child relationship, which lies outside the
signifier, but the passivity of the child creates anxiety at a certain point. The mother
becomes a 'threatening' mother (studies on hysteria show how the child experiences
fear of being killed/devoured by the mother).

"The attempt of the child to make the transition to the pole of activity must be understood as a running away from the position of passive object of enjoyment to an active form of pleasure." (Verhaege, 1999, p. 211.) For both sexes, the castration complex is fully implemented once the castration of the mother is discovered, which is
the moment that the mother loses her omnipotence. "The daughter turns away from
the mother to the phallophoric father with a definite goal: to acquire that which
could fill up the gaping desire of the mother, the lack of the first other." (Verhaege,
1999, p. 212.) In Lacanian terms, this means that the child leaves the imaginary and
enters the symbolic. Freud described this process as 'penis envy'. The way Lacan
would put it is that she 'turns' to the phallus (symbolic).

As Paul Verhaege (1999) explains, the child can only long for the mother and experience the Oedipus complex from a 'safe' place (within the active/symbolic order).
As the child enters the world of language, it realizes or feels that it is incomplete; it
cannot continue to be one and the same with the mother. The child has to obey the
law of the father, and cannot therefore have the mother. Moreover, it realizes that
neither itself nor the mother has the phallus; the father – who has the authority of
separating him from the mother – has it. The boy 'knows' he doesn't have it, but he
knows will have it (as his father does). As we can already see, the mother, in a
Freudian/Lacanian framework is not able by herself to guarantee either the meaning
or the autonomy of the subject. Indeed, separation from the symbiotic relation with
the mother (by the father) is a *sine qua non* condition for the child's entry into the
world of language. "The birth of the child has to be followed by the birth of the subject, or else the original intra-uterine relationship cannot be broken up." (Verhaege,
1999, p. 213.) The lack of separation would have the cost of either psychosis or perversion. Separation can only take place within the world of language. Language
then, constitutes a very ambivalent element in the life of the subject: on the one hand,
it permits inter-relation with the other in pact and symbol, but at the same time it
constitutes the tragedy of the individual – access to the sphere of the other and agreeing to live by the law of the word will mean the realization of the 'lack of being'; the

realization of incompleteness. The desire for the phallus, in this sense, means the desire for being, the desire for totality and completeness; the desire to annul the frontier separating the self from the other. The *Name of the Father* represents the *word* that makes that lack of being explicit, the one that shows the drama of having to assume separation from the mother. As such, it reveals the *desire* for the mother and at the same time shuts this desire away, as a repressed-unconscious desire. This process takes place regardless of the anatomical-biological difference between the sexes.

Sexual identification then does not respond to some kind of biological given, but takes place when the child enters the symbolic order, and basically consists of accepting having a phallus (in the case of the boy) or not having or being one (in the case of the girl). "We know that the unconscious castration complex has the function of a knot: (…) the installation in the subject of an unconscious position without which he would be unable to identify himself with the ideal type of his sex." (Lacan, 1977, p. 281.)

4   On Sexed Subjects: Fundamental Male and Female Fantasies

So what kind of resolution is achieved through the Oedipus complex? What does each gender's identity structure consist of? Sexual identity in Lacanian psychoanalysis has nothing to do with biology. It refers to the different positions (feminine/masculine) within language.

As we have seen, in order for the social being to emerge, repression has to take place, and in that sense, the *normal* way of being actually involves somehow being *sick*. As Freud taught us: "If you take up a theoretical point of view and disregard the matter of quantity, you may quite well say that *we are all* ill, that is neurotic – since the preconditions for the formation of symptoms (that is repression) can also be observed in normal people." (quoted by Fink, 2000, p. 77.)

A normal neurotic person (in their obsessive or hysterical modalities) is someone who has gone through repression, which means they have gone firstly through alienation (*jouissance* was given up and they joined the symbolic order) and secondly, separation (the lack was named, through separation from the mother's demand). The psychotic, on the other hand, has not entered the symbolic world *(the psychotic has no unconscious)*, and the pervert only went through alienation and not separation. The fundamental fantasy of the obsessive (typical masculine position) is desire for a relation with the object (the cause of desire or 'object *a*'), though they refuse to acknowledge that this object is related to the other. The hysterical (typical feminine position), on the other hand, fundamentally fantasizes about being the object of the other's desire. Therefore, obsessives actively negate and exclude the other, whereas hysterics restrict themselves to securing their subjective position (as long as they are wanted, their position is assured). Certainly these differentiations are not structural but contingent on our culture. Women are 'taught' to be the object of desire, whereas men are taught to be the conquerors of 'the thing'.

5   Sexed Enjoyment and Exclusion

If we accept that the symbolic order is structured around the signifier of the phallus (and therefore that there is an inherent incongruence between language, being and desire), then we have to agree that fantasy – defined as a transgressive narrative that both covers the inconsistency of an identity based on repression and puts desire in motion – is essentially male. The moral claims of restoration of social order, as well as ways of enjoying the exclusion of the other (both elements that characterize fantasy), are not gender neutral but represent both male moral claims (about the restoration of the threatened patriarchal order) and male forms of enjoyment. Some case studies inspired either by feminism or by psychoanalysis (or both) have indeed shown that the hatred of the other's way of enjoying (which is constitutive of social antagonism), is often expressed as misogyny. The study which goes furthest in this is Theweleit's (1987) study of fascism in Germany, through its analysis of the Freikorps' literary production. Though women were not directly the object of exclusion (it was communists first and Jews later), the excluded other represented a feminine threat, or as Jessica Benjamin puts it in the introduction to this book, "fear of feminine dissolution as opposed to male rigidity, erection and wholeness"[15].

Phallocentric logic, however, is not the only one which exists in a patriarchal society. Indeed, it allows for the development of different logics on the basis of the different positions that men and women have to the phallus. Since the structure of desire is common to everyone that goes through repression, Lacan differentiates the way men and women become subjects, again, according to their position with respect to the phallus or the main signifier.[16]

---

[15] See her introduction to Klaus Theweleit's, *Male Fantasies*, 1987.

[16] As Renata Salecl (2000) explains, the 'phallic signified' is the symbol of virility, penetrating power, the force of fertility and insemination, and so on. The 'phallic signifier' on the other hand, refers to the price the subject has to pay if he is to assume the meaning of the phallus. In this sense, Salecl continues, "the phallic signifier and symbolic castration are not opposed, but coincide. The phallic signifier is the direct signifier of symbolic castration." (p. 7.)

The feminine position involves not being fully inserted into the world of language; women are supposed to be linked more directly to what the symbolic order represses. This gives rise to *feminine jouissance*. Since no limitations are placed on them (women are not exposed to the threat of castration as men are since they know that *they don't have it, and they never will*) they may be closer to the real than men. For that reason, womanhood, it could be argued, represents the logic of inclusion. The logic of manhood, on the other hand, reflects the logic of exclusion. From that very distinction it could be argued that for men to enjoy, they have to transgress the symbolic order, and reach the realm of the drives. Women on the other hand, would not need to do so (or at least not in the same way), simply because they are constantly connected to the drives.

As has been argued by Julia Kristeva (1980, 1984), women transgress the symbolic order less than men, simply because they do not entirely subscribe to it.

Based on the contributions made to psychoanalysis by object theorists (in particular the work of Melanie Klein), Kristeva states that feminine logic governs the pre-Oedipal stage (before the constitution of language), and masculine logic governs the Oedipal stage (or the institution of the symbolic order). The pre-symbolic, or what she terms 'the semiotic', refers to the space where drives emanate and circulate. The symbolic order, on the other hand, consists of the procedures and organization of signification. Kristeva's distinction between the (feminine) semiotic and the (masculine) symbolic spheres is not enough to understand the presence/absence of violence, though it helps to show why the feminine is considered a threat to stability. A further differentiation is needed to account for the different types of disruption in the symbolic order.

6 On Asceticism, Mysticism and Dualism

Let me introduce Weber's typology of religion. In *Religious rejections of the world and their directions*, Weber (1958) presents three types of religious rationalities: the ascetic, the mystic, and the dualistic; three different routes on the quest for salvation. Asceticism – the world of Judeo-Christianity – is God-willed *action*, in which the believer is a tool of God, whereas mysticism – predominant in oriental religions such as Buddhism, Hinduism and Confucianism – focuses on a state of *possession-contemplation* of the sacred. In mysticism the individual is not a tool but a vessel of the divine. So, while the Judeo-Christian subject actively intervenes in the world to change it according to God's will, the mystic flees from the world. In dualism, the third form of religious rationality, "powers of light and truth, purity and goodness coexist and conflict with the powers of darkness and falsehood, impurity and evil" (Weber, 1958, p. 358). This dualistic logic was found in Zoroastrianism, in which the omnipotence of God was renounced and the existence of a great antagonistic force was acknowledged.

If one was to remain at the level of 'ideal types' (as Weber himself presented this typology), it could be argued that in the case of ascetic societies, violence has an ambivalent nature. On the one hand, it opens up space for social antagonism when intervening in the world and eliminating the other as a threat (which could take the form of any social group according to its race, religion, etc.). However, democracy (or the struggle for inclusion) is only possible within a certain framework of activism. Inequality and lack of freedom are combated in democracy, since they are considered to be the cause of suffering within the world.

Mystic societies on the other hand, while sublimating suffering, do not express violence against 'the other as threat'. However, lack of intervention in the world leads to quite a violent form of social organization, since deep social inequality and lack of freedom are not opposed either and social organization based on castes is a clear consequence of this type of solution. Unfortunately, Weber does not say much about dualism, which seems to present an interesting way of dealing with otherness; a boundary is established but at the same time it does not repress what is left out of the identity. According to Weber's account, this type of religious rationality has become part of historical experience: "the contemporary followers (the Parsees) have actually given up this belief because they *could not endure* this limitation of divine power" (Weber, 1958, p. 358). I think it is pertinent to link these types of religious rationality to Lacan's concept of sexual difference. It is certainly easy to establish a parallel between the purely ascetic way of dealing with otherness and the male type of insertion within the world of language; or one between dualistic religion and the female logic of being and not being in the symbolic world. As has been said, male insertion within the world of language represents a radical exclusion of part of it (its being), which cannot be represented in the symbolic order. What is left outside, however, continues to disrupt the symbolic order, and therefore must be opposed. Interestingly, Weber himself was well aware of the paradox of this type of rationality: while combating certain kinds of suffering, it is always creating new ones (what he called the conflict between substantial and formal rationality). The feminine identity – which is also part of the symbolic order – has no need to fear castration and would not need to repress that which is left out in the same way.

7 Concluding Remarks: Towards Feminine Ethics

Is the female way of insertion in language 'active' enough to fight for democracy? The answer to this question lies in the fact that the female way of insertion within the symbolic order is reflected not in the mystic religious rationality but in the dualistic one. The difference between the two is of great importance. In the mystic rationality there is a rejection of the world and the search for possession of the holy; in the dualistic, however, there is no rejection of the world order, but instead the recognition of different powers operating within it. "In the last analysis this dualism is only a direct systematization of the *magical pluralism* of the spirits with their division of good (useful) and evil (harmful)." (Weber, 1958, p. 358.)

Unlike Kristeva, I think it is necessary to stress the feminine presence in the world of language, and therefore its articulatory power. Since democracy needs activism in order to oppose exclusion, (which could be termed 'exclusion of exclusion'), we could say that it requires the presence of a feminine logic as opposed to purely male or artistic ones. The pure male logic would be one only of exclusion (a logic which guarantees the existence of society but which, working alone, is undemocratic and favors social antagonism). The pure artistic logic would be expressed as sublimation (which might produce beauty but is 'politically' passive). The female logic, on the contrary, is as active as the male logic, since it also experiences the rupture which occurs upon entry into the symbolic order and a first act of exclusion. However, as has been said, since women do not fear castration as men do, they still remain somehow connected to what has been repressed (the real). This lack of total rupture enables them to represent a more dualist being within language.

Women can, and indeed do, assume a male exclusionary logic once they are incorporated into established forms of power, and therefore discriminate against other less powerful or marginal groups (female homophobia is an example). The aim of democracy, or of inclusion, is far more than a mere quantitative increase in female participation in the public sphere. It is a radical qualitative change of logic, which is certainly a task for both men and women. Inclusion, however, will always remain in a dualistic logic of exclusion/inclusion, given the ambivalent nature of our being within language.

Transgression, sublimation and *feminine jouissance* then, would correspond to different ways of enjoying (outside the symbolic order) as the result of the inherent inadequate relation between language and being. Though transgression guarantees the existence of the symbolic order, it also brings violence and exclusion; exclusion as the primary act of the constitution of identity, and violence as the active repression

of what has been excluded. Sublimation would be a way of transforming the excluded energy into a work of art that could be appreciated within the social order. Its aim
would not be to eradicate the source of suffering, but to transform it into a source of
inspiration. Lastly, *feminine jouissance* – the starting point for *feminine ethics* – consists of the capacity to enjoy beyond the limits of the symbolic order, whilst not
breaking free from it, as is the case with transgression. *Jouissance* would not, however, mean total inclusion of being (or psychosis), since it does not entail the negation of the order of language, but only partial detachment from it. Though there is exclusion, there is no violence. The excluded element would not be fought against
since its presence would not constitute a mortal threat to the identity as such.

Probably the most sociological conclusion for this chapter would be to say that
each logic has its own function, and that each of them should have space assured
within society (or what Durkheim[17] might have called a 'good division of labor').
The male logic would guarantee the closure of the symbolic order (and the possibility of society), the female logic would provide the questioning of the established
meanings and boundaries of such society, and the artistic logic would ensure the possibility of producing beauty and entering the world of aesthetics. What remains clear,
however, is that predominance of the male logic in dealing with otherness does favor
violence and is inherently linked to exclusion (in order to exist) and to transgression
(in order to enjoy).

[17] See E. Durkheim, 1984.

Chapter 4: Democracy and Violence

I have argued that in order to theorize violence it is necessary to consider not only the contingent/historical character of particular expressions of violence, but also the more permanent/meta-historical character of social identities. It is thus necessary to look not only at the identities already constituted, but at the very process of constitution of social identities. Only then is it possible to see the *schism* (and exclusion) that is inherent in every social identity. This schism between the particular (the *empirico*/profane) and the universal (as the transcendental moral horizon which allows for the articulation of social life/sacred) is what accounts for both freedom and social change, and also for social antagonism. Social antagonism, expressed as social exclusion and violence, is a reaction to the fear of social disintegration; to the fear of the possibility of losing the universal/moral horizon that makes society possible.

I have argued that violence expresses a paradoxical dynamic between morality and enjoyment. Whilst violence is used in an attempt to restore the threatened symbolic order (that makes society possible), at the same time it also constitutes the ultimate transgression of that symbolic order.

The purpose of this chapter is to discuss the relationship between politics (defined as the political institutional arrangement of society) and social antagonism. In particular, the question that will be addressed here is whether the quasi-existential dynamic of social antagonism transcends the dynamics of politics, or whether it is possible for politics to *intervene* (preventing or fostering) social antagonism.

There are different ways of answering this question.

The first one is by stating the obvious: authoritarian regimes *per se* foster, openly legitimize and perpetuate social antagonism, while permanently and violently excluding those social groups, identities and activities that are seen as endangering the particular social project at stake from social/political life. Social antagonism *is* indeed the *modus vivendi* of authoritarian regimes; the enemy of authoritarian regimes can never die.

The second way of answering the question about the relation between politics and 'the political' is to state that, given the features of social and political life, not even democracies can avoid the emergence of social antagonism and violence. This would be based on the fact that democratic regimes also experience exceptional moments

when social antagonism (social exclusion and violence) is perceived not only as legitimate but also as the only way of 'keeping democracy safe' (i.e. a declaration of
war against another nation, the ban of certain political or social group from public
life, etc.). What is interesting to remember, however, is that this exception can take
place because there is a permanent war/intelligence infrastructure and national security ideology warning us about the possibility of an internal or external anti-demo-
cratic threat.

The most extreme case takes place when a democratic regime decides to interrupt
democracy by stopping all the mechanisms of democratic participation and declaring a state of internal war. This can take place when there is a generalized perception of imminent collapse, either in the shape of a threat of social anarchy, or a perceived totalitarian threat. For the Chilean case this type of analysis is of great importance, even though, paradoxically, the deepening of democracy in Chile actually led
to the military coup of 1973 and 17 years of dictatorship. As we will see in the second part of the book, a considerable part of the Chilean public *together* with the military gave up democracy for the sake of the 'basic constitutional principles' of the
country.

Does this mean then that democracy becomes irrelevant when considering social
antagonism?

No. On the contrary, it is *precisely* because of the constant possibility of conflict
that an open public sphere becomes absolutely necessary. As we saw in chapter 2, the
emergence of social antagonism *requires an enemy*; some 'other' has to embody a
mortal threat to the given society. In this way, discursive spaces in which both the
definition of identity and the definition of the other are deconstructed and compared,
and where new identifications may emerge, are indeed crucial. Through destabilizing fixed fantasies (or arbitrary constructions of others), these spaces might be able
to prevent the emergence of social antagonism. Although the negation of an excluded other would still occur to some degree, its survival would grant it the possibility
of later inclusion in the community.

We can try to go still further and ask what type or model of democracy can better
'understand' the nature of social antagonism and therefore, to a certain extent, con-
tain or prevent it? Or stated differently, what type of democracy has or creates fewer
enemies?

In order to answer this question, chapter 3 becomes very helpful. As we learnt
there, in our contingent (patriarchal) symbolic universe, social identities arebased
on two different principles: one that assures the closure of the system (which we
called masculine), and the other that subverts that closure (which we called

feminine). The presence of the first involves exclusion (of what threatens closure and the possibility of meaning), and the presence of the second guarantees inclusion.

Since we are not really dealing with the possibility of transcending the structural limits of patriarchal societies here (which would mean conceiving of the social order as structured by a first act of exclusion), we should at least take the function of each logic seriously when thinking about democracy: the male logic guarantees the closure of the symbolic order (and the possibility of society), the female logic provides the questioning of the established meanings and boundaries of society.

Historically, the political right – with its concern for social order and security – has played mostly a *masculine* function. The left, on the contrary, with its concern for social change and social inclusion, has played mostly a *feminine* function (when not in a position of power).

In order to answer the question about what type of democracy can better understand the nature of social antagonism and therefore prevent it, or what type of political organization creates fewer enemies, we can use this idea of dualism (or inclusion of two logics) as our first criterion and state the following: the predominance of the male logic favors social antagonism and is bound to exclusion (in order to exist) and to transgression (in order to enjoy); the greater the presence of the female logic in social organization, the smaller the fear of social disintegration, the greater the degree of social inclusion, and the less likely the emergence of social antagonism.

In what follows I will present two theories of democracy. One is Habermas's theory of the public sphere, and the other is the post-structuralist project of radical democracy. I will argue that Habermas's model of the public sphere is 'perniciously blind' to social antagonism. Though the whole purpose of his account is to get rid of power and violence, and instead establish an institutional mechanism for equal participation, his attempt to achieve universal validity and his ethical definition of political action can be seen as undermining democracy itself. His project seeks to foster a different other from that of power-exclusion (feminine-inclusion), yet his disavowal of libido (rationality is all that counts) and his universalist ethics (beyond the system of individuals' morals), mean that his project embodies the (masculine) voice of foundation, and therefore easily falls into the trap of social antagonism.

I will propose to work instead with the framework of radical democracy and the notion of hegemony. This theoretical perspective acknowledges the inherent logic of inclusion/exclusion that lies at the basis of the social, stresses the limits of every hegemonic project, and points out the very materiality of every articulation (as fixation/dislocation) in a system of meaning. The aim of cultural and political openness in this theoretical approach is precisely to *foster* this re-signification of meaning and the expansion of pluralism and social imaginaries.[18]

Most importantly, the notion of hegemony seems to incorporate the idea of dualism neatly. As we shall see in what follows, this notion incorporates the ambivalent logic of necessity and impossibility of the closure of society. Thus, ethics (previously conceptualized as the sacred) always remains contingent and dependent on how different normative orders are able to become the universal moral horizon of a community. In this scheme, democracy will consist precisely of the "possibility of keeping always open and ultimately undecided the moment of articulation between the particularity of the normative order and the universality of the ethical moment" (Laclau, in Butler, Laclau and Zizek, 2000, p. 86).

As we shall see, although Laclau's account deals quite well with one of the aspects of social antagonism (the political one), it misses two aspects which I consider fundamental. Firstly, the possibility that different identity structures might deal differently with excluded others, and secondly, the dynamic of enjoyment. In this respect Laclau's theory is certainly more adequate than Habermas's but he still does not fully conceptualize the experience of hate/jealously that is at the core of social antagonism and violence; the excluded other not only prevents my 'fullness', but is also the one who *prevents me from satisfying my desire, the one who steals my desire.*

1   Discourse Rationality

Habermas (1962) asked which conditions are necessary for a rational critical debate about public issues conducted by private persons willing to let arguments and not status determine decisions. This is a question regarding procedural rationality and the extent to which it can give credence to our views in the three areas of objective knowledge, moral practical insight and aesthetic judgment.

Habermas states that a public sphere adequate for democratic polity depends on both quality of discourse and quantity of participation (Calhoun, 1996). The criterion used to evaluate this adequacy is based on the distinction between strategic and communicative action. Strategic action is goal oriented and teleologically defined – it is termed successful when the goal is achieved – and is instrumental since the ac-

---

[18] In a situation of existing radical antagonism, however, this capacity of re-signification is very limited or non-existent. The identity of the excluded other is seen through a 'fixed fantasy' and its possibilities of 'talking back' are usually deprived of any symbolic power initially, and subsequently simply shattered physically.

tion is the means of achieving the goal. In communicative action, on the other hand, what matters is the understanding and agreement between those involved in the communication process. The actors know how to interpret the meaning of symbolic expressions and concur on how to act (these are only analytical distinctions, since both types of action generally take place together).

Within the realm of communicative action there are also sub-distinctions: on the one hand, what could be called 'simple communication' (there is a common background, therefore the actors involved in speaking do not need to explain and justify themselves in order to understand each other). On the other hand, Habermas poses discourse rationality. This is clearly different from strategic rationality which implies the use of appropriate means to achieve certain goals. Discourse rationality occurs when actors have to justify their statements to a much wider public than the narrow confines of their community's shared norms and ideas. Rational statements have to be supported by universal, rather than particularistic, ideas, norms and laws to which everybody would consent after examination in order to make them valid.

In his theory of communication, Habermas introduces the notion of an ideal speech situation, where it is not power but the features of free discourse which will define the outcome of the deliberation process. According to Habermas, the closer communication gets to this ideal speech situation, the closer knowledge comes to being universally grounded.

Avoiding some of the disappointing, totalitarian consequences of the philosophy of the enlightenment, Habermas stresses the importance of the process of operationalizing the notion of rationality; it is not the content of the 'truth' which matters as a test, but the formal procedure through which it is attained.

Obviously, the subject of the public sphere as presented by Habermas is a unitary subject, for whom knowledge and communication are unrestricted, so the task of universal pragmatics is to identify and reconstruct the universal conditions of possible mutual understanding (Habermas, 1998). Moreover, it is upon this unrestricted capability of the subject, that the whole edifice of the public sphere is built.

In this framework, one of the fundamental aspects of social antagonism, fantasy (the arbitrary construction of the other and the enjoyment of its exclusion), does not play any role. Public spheres, according to Habermas should be able to produce outcomes based purely on reasons. Prejudices, passions, misunderstandings, fears and jealousies do not belong in the political sphere. Even when Habermas used psychoanalysis as a model for social theory, he ended up abandoning the notion of libido entirely and, ultimately, the notion of the unconscious. In his account of psychoanalysis, therefore, Habermas missed precisely the nature of the unconscious (or radical other), reducing it to what can be translated (deciphered) into public language through inter-subjective communication. This can be criticized from both a Lacanian perspective[19] and from a Freudian one. As Joel Whitebook rather benignly states: "I am afraid that Habermas's linguistic reinterpretation of Freud has the effect of, as it were, destroying certain of Freud's central intentions in order to save them." (Whitebook, 1996.)

It is important to stress here too that Habermas's idea of universality (apart from entirely divorcing him from the symbolic interactionism in which he grounds his theory of communication[20]), introduces a very dangerous element for democracy. The other either disappears in the sameness of the self *(everybody will agree on certain reasons beyond cultural specificities)*, or, the other is condemned to represent a mortal/anomic threat to the republican principles of democracy. This argument becomes most forceful when *ethics* accompanies the universal. As we will see in what follows, the other has no other destiny than that of being the *immoral*.

We therefore have some idea of how this logic, whilst seeking to avoid social antagonism, literally follows its previously described development.

2 Discourse Ethics

In his essay *Morality and Ethical: Does Hegel's Critique of Kant apply to Discourse Ethics*, Habermas discusses the nature of moral knowledge. There he states that morality is a kind of safety device compensating for natural vulnerability in the individual's identity. From an inter-subjectivist approach, he states that individuals' identities are tied to the identities of other individuals, therefore they are vulnerable and in need of 'considerateness': "This explains the almost constitutional insecurity and chronic fragility of personal identity – an insecurity that is antecedent to cruder threats to the integrity of life and limb." (Habermas, 1999, p. 199.)

Moral intuitions allow us to behave best in situations where it is in our power to counteract the extreme vulnerability of others by being thoughtful and considerate. Habermas proposes the concept of 'cognitivist ethics', which he says can provide us with an answer to the question of how to justify normative statements. Discourse

---

[19] It is important to mention, however, that for a time Lacan also saw the possibility of de-alienation of the subject, and actually thought of the possibility of acquiring full speech: "The unconscious is that part of my history that is marked by a blank or occupied by a falsehood; it is a censored chapter." But the truth can be rediscovered; usually it has been written down elsewhere, *Function and field of speech and language* in Ecrits, 1977, p. 50.

[20] See Joas, *Pragmatism and Social Theory*, The University of Chicago Press, 1993.

ethics replaces the Kantian imperative by a procedure of moral argumentation: "only those norms may claim to be valid that could meet with the consent of all affected in their role as participants in a practical discourse". This ethical system is universal since it alleges that this (or a similar) moral principle, far from reflecting the intuitions of a particular culture, or epoch, is valid universally.

Habermas states that so far Mead and Rawls have also given answers to this question. For Rawls the impartiality of the moral point of view can be reached by the metaphor of the original position (or the veil of ignorance); for Mead, it is in the notion of role-taking. Discourse ethics, on the other hand, sets out the idea of argumentation (which assures that all concerned in principle take part, freely and equally, in a cooperative search for the truth, where nothing coerces anyone, except the force of the best argument).

According to Habermas, since moralities are tailored to suit the fragility of human beings individuated through socialization, they must always solve two tasks at once: they must emphasize the inviolability of the individual by postulating equal respect for the dignity of each individual, and they must also protect the web of inter-subjective relations of mutual recognition by which these individuals survive as members of a community. The principles of justice and solidarity correspond to these two complementary aspects respectively. While the first claims equal respect and equal rights for the individual, the second claims empathy and concern for the well-being of one's neighbor. According to Habermas, "all moralities coincide in one respect: the same medium, linguistically mediated interaction is both the reason for the vulnerability of socialized individuals and the key resource they posses to compensate for their vulnerability" (Habermas, 1999, p. 201).

Habermas seeks in this way to combine the benefits of a procedural definition of right with moral substance. "Moral discourse serves as a warrant of insightful will formation, insuring that the interests of the individual are given their due without cutting the social bonds that inter-subjectively unites them." (Habermas, 1999, p. 202.) Why does Habermas not ask about the vulnerability of inter-subjectivity itself? What would happen if he asked that question?

In order to answer this, we need to move on to his notions of legitimacy and legality and to his writings on civil disobedience.

3   Civil Disobedience

According to Habermas, since civil disobedience involves a transgression of the law, it appeals to something which goes beyond legality: legitimacy. For this reason, "civil disobedience must remain suspended between legitimacy and legality" (Habermas, 1985). However, though particular laws may be transgressed, what must always be respected is the constitutional order which embodies the principle of legitimacy. This for Habermas confines civil disobedience to the realm of *pacific* symbolic expressions.

Habermas states that acts of civil disobedience, or the "illegal acts carried out with appeal to the legitimating foundations of our democratic constitutional order" (Habermas, 1985, p. 99), are the true *guardians* of legitimacy. This is because civil disobedience works as a correction to the legal procedures of legislation and influencing legislation, and its goal is to make the law legitimate. In *Between Facts and Norms*, Habermas writes "the justification of civil disobedience relies on a dynamic understanding of the constitution as an unfinished project. From this long term perspective, the constitutional state does not represent a finished structure but a delicate and sensitive – above all, fallible and revisable – enterprise, whose purpose is to realize the system of rights anew in changing circumstances, that is, to interpret the system of rights better, to institutionalize it more appropriately, and to draw out is contents more radically. This is, the perspective of citizens who are actively engaging in realizing the system of rights. Aware of, and referring to, changed contexts such citizens want to overcome in practice the tension between social facticity and validity" (Habermas, 1998, p. 384).

Since they are legal, acts of civil disobedience are based on moral intuitions, and public spheres should use the presence of this external mechanism for evaluating identity between legitimacy and legality. Though risky, "in the last instance, the democratic constitutional state must rely on this guardian of legitimacy". Habermas is careful enough to describe the exceptional conditions under which civil disobedience is legitimate, and he is also careful to express that they are mostly symbolic expressions of moral insights which attempt to show peacefully the incongruence between the *de facto* law, and the principles of constitutional democracy. Although Habermas places legitimate civil disobedience within the constitutional framework (it should therefore be strictly peaceful), in light of my argument, civil disobedience, or the reaction of the political establishment, can easily become violent when there is the perception of a relation of antagonism (in other words, the perception of a relation of *either/or*), when the other (or enemy) has been demonized, and when social actors are capable of granting themselves the moral knowledge necessary to take the risk of *illegally saving society*.[21]

---

[21] In the case of the political establishment, closing down democratic mechanisms and acting *exceptionally* beyond the limits of the law.

Let us look at this possibility more closely. As we said previously, according to Habermas, both individuals and democracy are vulnerable. An individual's vulnerability is related to their mutual linguistic dependence,[22] whereas democracy's vulnerability is related to the historical incongruence between legitimacy and legality. In order to protect individuals, we have the safety device of morality and in order to protect democracy, we have that of civil disobedience. Habermas gives the example of the possible collapse of the representative system. In such a case, he states, "the nation as a collectivity of citizens, as well as individual citizens, must be permitted to assume the original rights of the sovereign. In the last instance, the democratic constitutional state must rely on this guardian of legitimacy" (Habermas, 1985, p. 105).

When Habermas states that civil disobedience must not transgress the constitutional order, he is stating (though indirectly) that this is vulnerable too. Legitimacy's other is anarchy (characterized by pure power without linguistic mediation). Habermas develops this argument by stating that civil disobedience has a place and is indeed legitimate in exceptional situations, but nonetheless those who disobey must take responsibility for their deeds. So when judging acts of civil disobedience, there can be different outcomes: a) they are considered successful when they effectively produce a change in the law and those responsible are not punished, b) they are considered mere crimes and are punished accordingly, c) civil disobedience is not only judged to be illegitimate but *immoral*. Civil disobedience is not seen as threatening a specific law, but the possibility of the law as such, and therefore, as leading to anarchy.

This is a very interesting case, precisely because what is questioned is the correct interpretation of legitimacy: on the one hand, there are those who disobey the law transgress in order to show the gap between the *de facto* law and legitimacy, and on the other, the political establishment which interprets that transgression as threatening legitimacy itself. So the question is *whose* moral insight is more adequate?

What is clear is that within Habermas's framework this is not a real dispute, just as the differential status between the law and legitimacy is not a real dispute either – there is a 'true' universal (permanent) principle of legitimacy, and a particular (historical) interpretation of it.

There are two ways in which this can be read regarding violence and legitimacy. One is to consider those who disobey as being legitimately 'violent' (since they

---

[22] Subjectivity emerges in a dialogue with others. Individuals are not self-sufficient but dependent on each other.

break the law in order to perfect democracy), and the other possibility is to understand violence as a legitimate reaction to a perceived threat against the constitutional order. In either case there is an appeal to a principle beyond the existing legality and in both cases there is an understanding of the exceptional nature of the situation.

Habermas states that "everybody involved should be part of the process of deliberation in the public sphere". However, in this situation this could obviously not be the case as the punishment or treatment of civil disobedience will not be discussed with the perpetrators themselves but imposed on them. This is where violence comes into play.

Though Habermas does not consider violence in this case, or if he considers violence it is from the perspective of those involved in civil disobedience, I think it is entirely logical to include it as a reaction to the anomic threat; the stronger the threat of anarchy, the greater the corrective mechanism, not only as exemplary punishment, but also as a measure to prevent further anarchy. This is the case of growing antagonism at the heart of societies (i.e. publics calling for military intervention, etc). So Habermas tells us that morality is a safety device for our own vulnerability and that civil disobedience is one for democracy. I would add that violence is also a safety device given the vulnerability of society and of inter-subjectivity.

4 Hegemony and Radical Democracy

As stated in the introduction of this last chapter, the best way of thinking of democracy requires the acknowledgment of two existing logics: one that assures power and continuity (which we called masculine), and another which allows for separation of power and subversion from existing meaning (or feminine). We stated before that the predominance a masculine logic leads to social antagonism, since this logic is based on exclusion. The pure presence of an inclusive logic, on the other hand, threatens the stability of the social. Authoritarian regimes, with their excessive concern for social order and homogeneity, attempt to negate this inclusive logic, and reduce the space of the indeterminate to a minimum.

Again, as made clear previously, we are not considering the possibility of transcending the structural limits of patriarchal societies here (which would mean not conceiving of the social order as structured by a first act of exclusion), but we are trying to think of how to make this society (with its structural limits) more inclusive, or more democratic and less antagonistic. We called this possibility dualism, and it consists first of all of the acknowledgment of the schism within society (because of the presence of a constitutive outsider), and therefore a greater capacity or flexibility to deal with that without the feeling of being mortally threatened. As stated in the previous chapter, exclusion still takes place, but the survival of the excluded other allows for the possibility of its later inclusion within the community. Simply stated, dualism recognizes the presence of a radical other, but it does not necessarily conceive of it as an enemy, so there is a smaller chance of a relation of antagonism being established with it.

When reflecting on democracy and the possibility of 'containing' the emergence of social antagonism it is important not only to have a theory of the social, but one for re-conceptualizing subjectivity itself. I have given elements of this kind of theory, mostly based on the notion of identification in chapters 2 and 3.

Let's see how the post-structuralist project of radical democracy faces these challenges.

As Laclau and Mouffe argue in their *Hegemony and Socialist Strategy* (1985), abandoning the category of the unitary subject as transparent and sutured entity, allows the specificity of the antagonisms constituted on the basis of different subject positions to be recognized, and, hence, the possibility of a deeper pluralist and democratic conception. These authors present their concept of hegemony as an alternative to any kind of collective action theory that departs from a 'foundationalist' point of view of man, politics and society. According to them, the foundation of politics in any universal moral value that defines essences and the understanding of politics as the expression of necessary laws lead to exclusionist and authoritarian versions of politics, since means and goals are pre-defined and not subject to further articulations.

The conclusions they reach about political life and the features of the radical democratic project depart from a theory of the subject and its relation to the symbolic order (or the field of language). Following Wittgenstein, Lacan and Derrida, they state that every object of the social world *emerges* in a discursive context, which gives a precarious and unfixed, relational meaning to their identities, which is not autonomous.

Discourse is understood as never reaching full articulation and as always part of a process of meaning displacement. Moreover, discourse is understood as material, and therefore producing effects over reality. This new understanding of discourse allows them to break with the traditional thought-reality dichotomy, and enlarges the field of social relations. Certainly it enlarges the notion of the public sphere from being a rational and separated moment of social life to an all-encompassing process of production and displacement of meanings and the social relations involved in them.

The subject, in this context, is never at the origin of social relations, but is an entity that emerges in such discursive conditions. The subject is also penetrated by the same ambiguous, incomplete and polysemical character that the symbolic-discourse mediation assigns to every discursive identity. This permanent change and the precarious character of social identities do not deny the possibility of thinking of democracy. On the contrary, according to Laclau and Mouffe, only when acknowledging this character of social reality, is it possible to think of a real democratic project: "It is the very lack within the structure that is at the origin of the structure. This means that we not only have subject positions within the structure, but also the subject as an attempt to *fill* these structural gaps. That's why we do not have just identities but rather identification." (Laclau, in Butler, Laclau and Zizek, 2000, p. 58.)

5 Articulation of Meaning and the Constitutive Outsider

The central point of Mouffe/Laclau is expressed in the concept of hegemony, which is broadly defined as the practice of articulation of plural discourses:

"The practice of articulation therefore, consists in the construction of nodal points which partially fix meanings; and the partial character of this fixation proceeds from the openness of the social, a result, in its turn, of the constant overflowing of every discourse by the infinitude of the field of discursivity." (Laclau & Mouffe, 1985, p. 113.) In this sense articulation is not articulation of thoughts or ideas, but articulation of social practices.

How does the production of hegemony take place?

According to the authors of *Hegemony*, the systematicity of the system of meaning works provided that it is a closed system. However, it is also necessary to contemplate what is outside the system, that which is not only another difference within it, but an element of *antagonism*, with which there is a relation of dialectical opposition. The presence of an element outside the system of meaning not only produces alienation for the subject, but also accounts for the instability of the social. Whilst at the individual level we can speak of an unconscious which is irretrievable by language, at the social level it is possible to speak of antagonism, which has quite similar disruptive potentialities. This basic presence of an outside element defines the limits of the system and at the same time prevents its complete closure. The outside element is actually beyond the system. In Laclau and Mouffe's terms, this means that the outside element constitutes the condition of possibility of the system at the same time as it constitutes its impossibility.

Among the elements which participate within the system, and relate to the external element in the same exclusionary way, a relation of *equivalency* is constituted; though each of their identities is different, they are analogous in their relation of exclusion with the same outsider. The increase in the logic of equivalence among them, however, involves a process of emptying of meaning, a decrease of difference between them, and the emptying gives an opportunity for one of the elements of the system to represent (though inadequately) its totality. This is what Laclau later calls the "empty signifier" (1996).

The logic of hegemony consists precisely of the power to over-determine the meaning of the elements (originally in a situation of dislocation or instability) at play. Hegemony only refers to a *provisional* form of power, where certain modes of articulating discourses and social reality dominate others, in which *partial and temporal* agreements are achieved.

6   The Universal

The concept of the universal is fundamental for the understanding of the hegemonic process. As Laclau states, if a particular group in society can represent (inadequately) the totality, this means that power in society is uneven. Moreover, he states "there is hegemony only if the dichotomy universality/particularity is superseded; universality exists only if it is incarnated in – and subverts – some particularity, but, conversely, no particularity can become political without also becoming the locus of universalizing effects" (Laclau, in Butler, Laclau and Zizek, 2000, p. 56).

Laclau states that the universal can be conceptualized in two different ways. The first one involves the dissolution of all particularity and corresponds to Marx's idea of (total) human emancipation where there is a re-encounter of history with human nature. In this first case – of non-mediated universality – power becomes superfluous since civil society realizes its being in and for itself. In the same way, it is possible to state that mediation is not necessary: the universal is the expression of an essence which needs nothing external to itself to be what it is.

A second way of conceptualizing the universal is to understand it as a contingent universal: particularity is not dissolved, but the universal is a "consequence of a partial section of civil society achieving general domination" (Laclau, in Butler, Laclau and Zizek, 2000, p. 44). In this case the universal is achieved by passing through the particular. "Something which does not cease to be particular has to demonstrate its right to identify its own particular aims with the universal emancipatory aims of the community." (Ibid, p. 46.) For Marx this type of universal corresponds only to partial or political emancipation, where one class represents the interests of the whole society.

Contrary to the first conceptualization of the universal, in this case power is all but irrelevant. Any potential universalizing effect is seen as depending on the antagonistic exclusion of an oppressed sector, which means that power and political mediation are inherent to any universal emancipatory identity. For this to happen two mediations are necessary. The first corresponds to the transformation of the particularistic of the rising dominant sector in the emancipatory discourse of the whole society, and the second is the presence of an oppressive regime which is the very condition of that transformation.

"The elimination of all representation is the illusion accompanying the notion of total emancipation. But, in so far as the universality of the community is achievable only through the mediation of a particularity, the relation of representation becomes constitutive." (Ibid, p. 57.) Laclau's view is that the universal relies not only on the collapse of all particularities, "but on a paradoxical interaction between them" (Ibid, p. 56).

7   The Political Field

Having described the logic of the social in this way, the obvious conclusion is that a political dimension is constitutive of all social identity. This is quite a significant statement since it fosters the blurring of the demarcation line between state and civil society. For Laclau the idea of a totally emancipated and transparent society, from which all *tropological* movement between its parts would have been eliminated, involves the end of all hegemonic relations and with it, the end of democratic politics. Thus democracy is simply the enactment or facilitation of this permanent displacement of meanings and the formation of new hegemonic relations.

But where does politics or democracy take place? According to Laclau and Mouffe the entire social life entails political relations. They argue that every notion is not only relational but also ideological: the content of the signified (meaning) which is going to be attached to each signifier (concept) is matter of political contestation. The signifying process involves the whole of the social life, therefore politics is not only the deliberating process; on the contrary, at the very heart of politics is the production of meanings.

Their democratic project proposes to keep the democratic contestation alive, to recognize the contingent nature of politics (or the political character of politics), the opening of spaces for the expression of conflicts, and the recognition of the exclusion that every form of power entails. "When we accept that every consensus exists as a temporary result of a provisional hegemony, as a stabilization of power, and that it always entails some form of exclusion, we can begin to envisage democratic politics in a different way. A democratic approach that thanks to the insights of deconstruction, is able to acknowledge the real nature of its frontiers and recognizes the forms of exclusion that they embody, instead of trying to disguise them under the veil of rationality or morality, can help us to fight against the dangers of complacency." (Mouffe, 1996, p. 10.)

As we can see, a democratic theory based on the notion of hegemony does not fall into the same traps that made Habermas's theory unwillingly reproduce the logic of social antagonism. The new conceptualization of the *contingent universal*, the expansion of politics from the rational debate to all social practices, the renunciation of the idea of moral progress and the recognition of a constitutive outsider are the most salient conceptual achievements of Laclau and Mouffe.

The concept of hegemony definitely fosters democratic politics and opens our eyes to the imminent power relations which are constitutive of society. As we saw in the last section of this chapter, instead of attempting to prevent the existence of power or dismantle it, this theory recognizes it as foundational. The unavoidable character of power is made present even where it appears as non-existent (because of consolidated hegemonic relations).

Laclau proudly positions his theory beyond the realm of sociology (a discipline which is only capable of describing already constituted identities) in order to be able to grasp the logic inherent in the constitution of every social identity. However, merely understanding the logic of exclusion/inclusion which is at the heart of the social antagonism dynamic fails to answer some relevant questions: Are all identity structures the same? Do they relate in the same way with what they exclude? What triggers the emergence of violence? How does the jump between symbolic exclusion to physical violence take place?

Laclau and Mouffe give a general answer by stating that it is not possible to know where social antagonism is going to emerge, because there is a permanent displacement of meaning. Though I agree with this statement, I think it is possible to go a bit further than that, especially when feminist theory and psychoanalysis are integrated into the analysis. The theory of hegemony does not do that and their incorporation of Lacan can be largely reduced to the idea of the ambivalence and impossibility of fully constituted identities, and leaves out the impact of the drive and desire. The result is that this theory ends up being disembodied, which is exactly what violence and social antagonism are not about.

In that respect, I consider the work of Zizek quite ground-breaking. Like Laclau, he is conceptualizing a theory of the social but fully acknowledges the drive when he proposes to work with the notion of fantasy.

Is it possible to answer these questions from the perspective of the logic of the constitution of the social, or is it necessary to look at already constituted identities? I think that even within the pure language of the logic it is possible to advance further. As I have suggested in chapter 3, gender could be considered as a category for differentiating identity structures and therefore different ways of dealing with otherness (or the excluded) and of enjoying exclusion. However, from the realm of already constituted identities (so from a sociological perspective) we can learn not only about the specifics of particular antagonistic relationships, but also about, if not the necessary, at least the sufficient discursive elements that antecede the emergence of social antagonism expressed in violence against the excluded other.

Perhaps Mouffe wanted to move in that direction (one less 'blindly' existential than Laclau's) when she put forward the theory of agony. The question Chantal Mouffe asks is not how to arrive at a consensus without exclusion (since this would imply the eradication of the political), but how to transform an enemy into an adversary – in other words, an enemy which is seen as legitimate.

8   Conclusions: Ethics and Politics

Within social theory and philosophy the notion of *necessity* has always been the *positive and certain* standpoint from which a normative definition about the essence of human nature allows us to have a critical judgment about the actual development of history and society. The classical examples in this respect are the philosophies of history developed by Hegel and Marx, and the classical Frankfurt School. More recent theoretical developments (particularly in the field of political theory), have tried to reconcile necessity – and keep a normative model which otherwise is unthinkable – and contingency, incorporating the developments of hermeneutics and symbolic interactionism, as in the contributions made by Honneth (1996)[23] and Habermas (1984).

---

[23] A little more than ten years after Habermas published his *Theory of Communicative Action*, Axel Honneth presented *The Struggle for Recognition*, in which he attempted to give substance to what he saw as an excessively abstract and formal definition of the public sphere. According to Honneth, the communicative model presented by Habermas lacked the foundations to define it as a *morally motivated struggle*, which according to him, has to accompany the description of human conflict. Mostly based on Hegel's early writings, but also on the work of G. H. Mead and D. Winnicott, Honneth presented his threefold model of recognition, 'love, rights, and esteem', which account for potential motivation of social conflict.

For both theorists, since agreement and understanding stand for the foundational moment in the constitution of the social, a particular model of communication becomes the normative pillar from which society can be critically judged.

These normative theories of democracy have attempted to set out the conditions under which greater social inclusion and participation can be achieved. From prescriptions of formal procedures of equality of participation to moral claims about the need for greater tolerance, philosophers and political theorists envisage a society where violence and exclusion can be avoided. *The power of the word over the power of the deed*, so they say. Communication and understanding, these liberals argue, are the key conditions that can prevent naked power (or violence) from taking over society, and can ensure instead that justice (all individuals have the same worth) and solidarity (individuals are vulnerable and need recognition) can be achieved. It is hard to disagree with the outlined political/democratic motivation of this approach, and indeed they are right when they say that *while there is communication* (as long as subjects are indeed speaking to each other), *overt social antagonism or violence do not occur*. Actually, violence is characterized by the silencing of those who are being abjected; put differently, violence does not expect a reply.

This, however, is not all that is at stake in this project. As we saw in this chapter, though Habermas escapes the monological and aprioristic character of Kantian morality, he still asserts that individuals, in an ideal speech situation, could reach inter-subjectively universal validity claims. Moral insights and universal validity claims, though, are definitely close to the experience of mastering the foundation, and, as explained in chapter 2, violence (at least in modern societies) is always preceded by this kind of universal and moral discourse. The language of social antagonism is fundamentally a moral (masculine) language, and the enemy always represents 'evil'. In this respect, I argued that I agree with Chantal Mouffe when she states that "the democratic character of society can only be given by the fact that no limited social actor can attribute to herself or himself the representation of the totality and claim to have the mastery of the foundation" (Mouffe, 2000, p. 100).

Furthermore, I consider that Habermas's cognitive ethics do not leave room for understanding otherness. His account not only fails to conceptualize *radical otherness*, but even simple otherness or difference ends up being subsumed by the sameness of the self. This conceptual shortcoming prevents Habermas from seeing how the process of social antagonism arises, or how the very public sphere – (mis)using his conceptual tools – can even foster it. Though to a certain extent Habermas conceptualizes the schism between the *empirico* and the transcendental dimensions that characterize social life (mostly expressed in the dichotomy legality/legitimacy), he does not see this schism as a possible source of social antagonism, but as an opportunity for true autonomy.

Morality and rationality will eventually allow us to bridge the gap between facticity and validity, Habermas states.[24] An entirely different conception of the relation between politics, normativity and ethics is presented by Laclau.

While in Habermas's writings, politics is the means by which facticity (or the particular normative order) and validity (as the real-universal ethical truth) can be reconciled once and for all, in Laclau's version politics must always take the constitutive incongruence between those terms into account; hegemony is the way of naming this unstable relation between the ethical and the normative.

The starting point of this approach regarding ethics is the entirely different conception of the universal presented above. The universal is not the expression of the dissolution of all particularities, but – being a contingent universal which acts as the horizon of all the particulars – it is simply the result of a hegemonic process of production of meaning (or what Laclau calls the 'production of empty signifiers'). The ethical is the moment of universality of the community, "the moment in which, beyond any particularism, the universal speaks by itself" (Laclau, in Butler, Laclau and Zizek, 2000, p. 80).

According to Laclau, the distinction is not between descriptive and normative but between the ethical (in his words, "as the moment of madness in which the fullness of society shows itself as both impossible and necessary") and the descriptive/normative complexes which "are the ontic raw materials incarnating, in a transient way, that universality – that elusive fullness".

Laclau states that there is an ethical *investment* in the normative because no normative framework is *per se* ethical. Let us look at this more closely. So far we have two different versions. In the first one the normative and ethics coincide (Habermas). In this case, Laclau states that there is no real investment, or no decision, since it is essentially the expression of an underlying nature. In the second version, there is a decision. Not pure decisionism, however, because in such a case there is no acknowledgment of the existing limits of a decision, i.e. the existing normative orders. For Laclau, "hegemony is a theoretical approach which depends on the essentially ethical decision to accept, as the horizon of any possible intelligibility, the incommensurability between the ethical and the normative (the latter including the de-

---

[24] It is interesting to know that Habermas believes that history is indeed moving towards that end, not because of the Hegelian absolute spirit, but because of concrete historical social movements.

.scriptive)" (Ibid, p. 81). This brings us back to the subject: "the subject who takes the decision is only *partially* a subject; he is also a background of sedimented practices organizing a normative framework which operates as a limitation on the horizon of options" (Ibid, p. 83).

Again, according to Laclau, this decision to accept the contingency or partiality of the universal is fundamental for democracy: "If a community is to be a democratic one, everything turns around the possibility of keeping always open and ultimately undecided the moment of articulation between the particularity of the normative order and the universality of the ethical moment. Any full absorption of the latter by the former can lead either to totalitarian unification or the implosion of the community through a proliferation of purely particularistic identities." (Ibid, p. 86.)

Chapter 5: Outline of a Theory of Violence

I have argued that recognition (or inter-subjectivity) has an intrinsic limit and that in given circumstances the relation with the other is entirely ruled by fantasy. This means that the self and the other will not only 'mis-recognize' each other, but they will attempt to destroy each other in an attempt to save themselves from the threat the other poses to their existence. From this analytical perspective, although the relation with the other is always marked by a certain degree of invention about who the other is and what it wants, the process of becoming an enemy and the relation of antagonism and hate that would characterize that process is based on the negation of the other and the enjoyment of its exclusion. In this case desire is not experienced as mutual recognition (or mutual satisfaction), but is expressed as a relation of aggressive jealousy – the desire of the other opposes my desire, denies my desire in such a way that it denies and excludes 'me', my identity. I have also argued, however, that not every social identity is equally exposed to radical antagonism and that not every threat to the identity results in violence.

Why is this? Because though every fantasy produces some type of enjoyment, not every fantasy involves relations of antagonism and violence. On the contrary, different identity structures and different fantasies seem to allow for the existence of different relationships with what has been excluded, and some of them are more violent and others non-violent. As I argued in chapter 2, the more patriarchal the society, the more likely the emergence of violence against the excluded other. This is the case because in patriarchy the other seems to threaten the male identity more easily, and transgression – which is linked to violence – is the masculine type of enjoyment.

However, even within patriarchal social organizations, male fantasies do not necessarily lead to violence. Indeed, social antagonism, expressed in the hostility towards and exclusion of others, can acquire different forms and contents, and can reach different levels of violence. It can be expressed as cultural exclusion (socially, not legally, penalized taboos), partial legal exclusion (lack of certain rights), total exclusion (physical violence), etc., depending on the type of fantasy that defines the identity and its relation to the other.

We can say at this point that the definition of the excluded group and the type of exclusion that will be enacted against it will depend on the power relations and hegemonies existing in society, and the type of fantasies surrounding them. Deeply established hegemonies and fantasies do not usually change overnight. On the other hand, it is important to keep in mind that hegemonies are no more than provisional articulations of otherwise dislocated elements.

So, the question that remains to be answered is: What type of fantasy about the self and the other antecedes violence? What type of definition of the self and definition of the other enable the taboo of violence to be lifted in societies where the rule of law and democratic procedures of negotiation have been accepted as the legitimate means of dealing with conflicts? In order to answer this question let me start by summing up the most important elements of the theories I have discussed in the previous chapters:

1   Violence as Constitutive of Society

Violence is constitutive of our society. It is the expression of a necessary act of exclusion that takes place in the process of the constitution of the social identity. An antagonistic relationship is established in the process of identity formation between the identity and what needs to be excluded from it for the identity to exist. This first foundational act of exclusion is cast in positive terms by a transcendental narrative about the identity, which Castoriadis has called 'the social imaginary'. Since the stability of the identity relies on this exclusion, any threat to the boundary of the identity, from within or without, elicits a (probably violent) response from the identity against the apparent cause of its instability. The transcendental narrative provides the identity with the moral legitimacy to attack what threatens it and restore social order.

2   Identification and the Libidinal Link with Ideal Self

The psychoanalytical notion of identification allows us to understand the process of emergence of the self (or social identity), and also the libidinal relation the self establishes with the transcendental narrative about itself and about the excluded other. The process of formation of the self, in its primordial alienation, is related to a process of fixation and development of a *passion for being* according to the ideal self that corresponds to its imaginary identification. The notion of identification allows us to go beyond the concept of meaning and rationality, and instead the notion of a 'de-centered' subject is introduced; a subject whose motivations for action are not only conscious and preconscious, but also unconscious. According to the psychoanalytical theory of identification, the self is not closed in itself but is given to the other from its very beginning. The self's definition will depend on the images that it will incorporate from the exterior. Unlike the case of a purely Foucauldian post-structuralist perspective, however, the psychoanalytical subject never belongs to the other, but keeps its unconscious as the space of resistance.

3   Fantasy

By taking quite a different perspective from that of crowd behavior theorists, I want to recover the non-rational/non-social (neither strategic nor learnt) component of violence, and discover its internal logic and meaning. I will do so using the psychoanalytical notion of fantasy. Fantasy plays a crucial role in the constitution of the social identity and seems to dissolve the previous existing dichotomy in the literature of violence (meaning/rationality vs. irrationality). On the one hand, fantasy provides the identity with a transcendental narrative; an idea of wholeness which conceals the inconsistency – and arbitrary nature – of the formation of the social which contributes to the stability of a particular system of meaning. The transcendental narrative about the identity is also a narrative about the apparent cause of its instability: a narrative about a pernicious other is also constructed. Unlike a pragmatist account of the intersubjective relation (where the self and the other emerge together in a mutual dialogue) the notion of fantasy stresses the arbitrary content of both, the definition of the self and the definition of the other, and the limits of communication. In this way, once a certain other has been labeled as the enemy, or as the element that prevents the identity from fully realizing itself, the other has little (if any) chance of changing its imposed status.

The libidinal tie between the subject and its transcendental narrative, and between the subject and the other, bring us to the dynamic of enjoyment. According to the basic postulates of psychoanalytical theory, the possibility of society lies in a foundational act of repression of the drives (pleasure and death drives). In Lacanian terms, it could be said that though the subject is "given from the start to the other" (to language), a space of pure being always remains un-linguistified (or non-socialized). This is the subject's unconscious. Fantasy links the subject with its drives, and allows it to enjoy, which is why fantasy constitutes a social way of transgressing the moral order.

Discursively, fantasy attempts to explain the failure of the subject at the same time as projecting this failure into the other (where the other is accused of wanting to do what the self is actually doing or wants to do). The relation established between the self and the other is a relation of jealousy of the other's enjoyment, which is usually cast as disgust at the other's way of enjoying. The excluded other is accused of 'stealing the enjoyment of the self'. The dynamics of hate seem to spring from this type of relation with the excluded other.

4   Fantasy and Sexuality

Collective violence (at least in modern societies) not only seeks the restoration of social order, but the restoration – or reinforcement – of masculine law or patriarchal social order. Such social order dictates a particular mode of enjoyment *(phallic jouissance)* as a particular form of transgressing the law. That is, violence and exclusion will be regarded here as expressions of a masculine way of enjoying the transgression of the symbolic order and, paradoxically, as ways of restoring such an order. In this framework the excluded other *par excellence* is feminine desire, associated in our masculine culture with passivity and disintegration.

5   Elements of a Violent Fantasy

The double nature of fantasy (its relations to meaning and enjoyment) is expressed discursively in the presence of two kinds of elements: one, clearly discursive and always outspoken, is characterized by the moral justification of violence; the other, more hidden but still present in the relation with the other, is characterized by the experience of enjoyment. These two elements, morality and enjoyment, are articulated in four discursive formations characterized by the presence of: universality, antagonism, sexuality and hate.

a)   Universality

This dimension describes the equating of the stability of society to the stability of a particular identity. This provides the threatened identity with a moral discourse that legitimizes its violence against the other. This type of legitimacy is usually found in state violence, national security type of discourses (Weber, 1978; Katzestein, 1996) and political violence (Apter, 1997). I have used the term 'universal' because this type of discourse denies the presence of any other foundational or regulating principle of social life.

b) Antagonism

This dimension describes the denial of the possibility of negotiation. This is the most considered variable when analyzing the root of violent conflicts, and has usually been reduced to antagonistic visions of society (Subercaseaux, 1997).

c) Sexuality

This dimension describes the amoralization, or hypersexualization of (at least one) of the identities. It is experienced as disgust for the other's way of enjoying (Salecl, 1996). When one of the identities steps out of morality (and becomes violent) in order to defend the morality that protects society, it fights against an enemy which is portrayed as evil, an enemy which it must eradicate. This attribute of fantasy is particularly evident in cases of hate crimes – motivated by homophobia or racism – where the victim is morally judged on their pernicious way of enjoying (Kelly & Maghan, 1998).

d) Hate

This dimension describes the possibility of enjoying the suffering of the other. This is the most problematic dimension of a violent fantasy, because this enjoyment is never fully admitted by the actors of violence (Zizek, 1997), though it seems a crucial variable when trying to understand (non-strategic) excesses of violence.

It seems reasonable to state that the presence of all these elements in a relation of antagonism (or the absence of some of them) in a context of violence, is related to the degree of moral constitution (or cohesiveness) of the community within which such antagonism takes place (Durkheim, 1984).The stronger the social bond, the more attributes need to be present for physical violence to emerge. On the contrary, the weaker the social bond (as in anomic societies), the fewer attributes need to be present in a relation of antagonism for physical violence against people to emerge.

Second Part:

The Meaning of Anti-Communism in Chile

Chapter 6: Historical Fantasies: The Right and Left in Chile

In this chapter I will briefly present the major political events that took place in Chile during the 20th century and look at the context that surrounded the political crisis at the beginning of the seventies. It will be stated that the identity structures – and therefore the fantasies – of the Chilean left and right were quite dissimilar. Whereas the right often appealed to universalism (presenting itself as the only political tendency capable of providing the basis for the Chilean social and moral order), the left remained mostly reformist (by asking not about the foundations of the moral order but about ways of improving the existing order).

The political right lost the power it had historically held in the country in the elections of 1938. Different elements contributed to the emergence of a new power arrangement. The first one to mention is the change in the organization of the political system, which became characterized by a tendency towards the concentration of parties (instead of their atomization), the rise of a competitive left with increasing electoral support, and a center with extensive capacities for consensus (which indeed became the axis of the party system). The second main factor that contributed to this new power configuration was the ultra-liberal nature of the political discourse of the right itself. The right at the time proposed and supported the doctrine of individualism and the predominance of market laws, assuming that human nature aimed for the maximization of profit (Moulián & Torres, 1985). Supported by the Chilean upper class, the economic interests of the political right lay in the agrarian model and it promoted minimal state participation in it. However, given the open economic crisis at the time, this project was seen as 'anti-modern' by the middle classes, who thought it was necessary to come up with and promote an alternative project for the development of the country based mainly on industrialization.

The new arrangement of the political system together with the new economic project for the country led to the electoral victory in 1938 of the progressive coalition of the Popular Front, led by the secular Radical Party *(Partido Radical)*. This party stayed in power for three consecutive presidential terms (1938, 1942 and 1949).

Radicalismo was characterized throughout the period by the lack of ideologism and its stress on the social and economical functions of the state. The state had no totalitarian tendencies but was a service-state that sought to complement private initiatives intended to promote the general interest of society (Urzúa, 1987). During these decades, the state promoted industrial development and the creation of the necessary institutions in order to achieve it. The Radical Party period is described as promoting integration and democratization of the country. [25],[26]

The historical political alliance (center-left) was broken in the last radical party government, and the right once again won the presidency in 1958. In 1964, however, fearing the victory of the socialist candidate, the right supported the Christian democrats, who won the presidential elections with an absolute majority. During this period, significant reforms to the political system were promoted and the electorate grew considerably. Important economic reforms were also introduced, with the Agrarian Reform being the most important of them (Yocelevsky, 1987). This was experienced by the landholders (and the political right in general) as the greatest violation of individual rights in Chilean history up to that moment.

The following political period (1970–1973), was led by the leftist Popular Unity coalition (*Unidad Popular* [UP]). It was formed by most of the leftist parties existing at the time, with the communist and socialist parties as its constituent nucleus and Salvador Allende as the president of the country.[27] The political differences between the two main parties – the former more reformist and the latter more revolutionary – generated a high degree of tension in the government. Redistribution was one of the main objectives of this government and this was carried out through the socialization of hitherto unaffected private assets (such as banks and industries).

The difference between this short socialist period and the previous ones is that policies were intended to redistribute not only goods but also economic and political power; to abolish – or at least greatly diminish – the private hold on the means of production. These policies were defined as revolutionary, in opposition to the previ-

---

[25] Such as the incorporation of women into the electorate in 1949.

[26] Another characteristic of the period is that because of the large increase in social expenditure, the state got into serious difficulties since taxation levels were insufficient, so from the beginning of the fifties, it was necessary to apply anti-inflationary politics.: MIDEPLAN, *"Evolución de las Políticas Sociales en Chile, 1920–1991"*, Documentos Sociales, Santiago, 1991.

[27] It is important to mention here that in 1967 the Socialist Party had adopted the *"Rebelión Popular"* thesis, where armed and revolutionary methods were accepted as legitimate. This did not avoid its political alliance two years later with the Communist Party, which had followed the opposite route till then, since it had adopted constitutional and electoral methods of struggle to achieve socialism. Smaller left-wing parties of the time such as *Radical, Social Demócrata, Movimiento de Acción Popular Unitario* y *Acción Popular Independiente* also participated in the *Unidad Popular* coalition.

ous reformist ones. This period was the last in which all public policies were formulated by the state, and the last in which the state was the sole structure responsible for the welfare of population.

1 Background to the Presidential Elections in 1970

The historical Chilean electoral scheme of 'three thirds' was once again enacted in 1970 with three presidential candidates each representing one of the political tendencies of the moment. Jorge Alessandri, Radomiro Tomic and Salvador Allende competed against each other, and each of them got around a third of the votes. The alliance of the left was a broad political alliance of Marxist-Leninist parties together with leftist Christians and other small parties that favored an economic structural change for Chile. In total there were six parties involved, with the socialist and communist parties at the head of the coalition. The right was represented by the National Party (together with a smaller Radical Democracy Party), and the center was mostly represented by the Christian Democrat Party [PDC].

It is important to remember that during the late sixties Chile's social, economic and political power structures were under considerable pressure. Not only was the leftist electorate growing, as new voters were incorporated into the political system, but landowners were having their land expropriated. At the time, the revolutionary left (*Movimiento de Izquierda Revolucionaria* [MIR]) had carried out bank robberies and some armed attacks in Santiago, and a wave of strikes in different mining sectors and agricultural sectors was hitting the country. The social climate of deep changes and the festive spirit of the lower classes and marginal sectors of society, which were acquiring new forms of power and political representation, were experienced as a source of great uncertainty and social disorder.

Moreover, the international context was also politically threatening for the right. The success of the Cuban revolution and the growth of guerrillas in neighboring countries (such as *Tupamaros* in Uruguay, *Montoneros* in Argentina and *Ejercito de Liberación Nacional* in Bolivia), made the power of the Soviet Union appear stronger and closer to South America; the enemy was now within national boundaries. Chilean anti-communist ideology did not differ from the American anti-communism that characterized those years.

This political climate of confrontation made the right set out its presidential campaign as a very aggressive crusade against 'the communist threat'. Their program contemplated social welfare, favored strong government and stressed the need to reduce social expenditure and support private capital, without entirely dismantling the existing mixed economy.

The political program of the Popular Unity Party [UP], the left-wing coalition, on the other hand, offered 'to begin the construction of socialism in Chile' and stressed economic measures, especially changes in property relations. Regarding agriculture, Allende's program included the deepening of the Agrarian Reform initiated by the previous Christian democrat government. The most controversial measures, however, proposed the creation of a 'socialized' sector in the economy (still keeping private ownership and mixed ownership of means of production), the nationalization of foreign-owned copper, nitrate, iron and coal mines, banks and other companies involved in foreign commerce, and other enterprises considered critical for Chilean economy (transport, communication, etc.) were also to be socialized according to the UP's program.

The second big issue in the program was the creation of a one-house legislature ('a popular assembly') to replace the existing two-house legislature. Thirdly, the program contemplated the creation of a unified educational system [ENU]. Of course important welfare measures, from the distribution of half a gallon of milk per child, tax exemptions for small houses, to the disbanding of the police riot squad, were also included.

Finally the UP stressed that the government would be a multi-party government, would respect the rights of the opposition, and would govern within the boundaries of existing Chilean legality.

Tomic's program was rather close to the UP's program (it also included the nationalization of copper). Tomic was also attacking and attempting to change the existing capitalist system and foster a new economy, which would be financed by a Fund for National Independence and Development based on copper revenues, individual and group savings and new taxes for high-income groups. Politically, however, Tomic was closer to Alessandri, since he also proposed strengthening the power of the president.

The percentage results of the presidential elections were as follows: Salvador Allende 36.3; Jorge Alessandri 34.9; Radomiro Tomic 27.8. The Christian democrats recognized Allende's victory, but the right did not and chose to wait until the last minute for the decision of the congress. According to Chilean law, if there was no absolute majority (50% + 1) the congress had to choose between the first two candidates who obtained most of the votes.

Between election day and nomination day the social climate of the country was deeply affected by violence. Faced with the possibility of Allende's nomination, the CIA and right-wing Chilean military planned the kidnapping of Rene Schneider, the chief of the military, who was seen as an obstacle for a coup against Allende. As is well known, since Schneider defended himself, this initial attempt at kidnap ended up in his murder.

The Christian Democrat Party asked the UP to give specific 'constitutional guarantees' before they would support Allende's presidential nomination. Their justification in so doing was that they wanted to assure the survival of the constitutional state. According to the UP, Allende's political program already included such guarantees. The UP's answer was considered unsatisfactory so Allende had to sign a document anyway guaranteeing respect for the constitution and its continued existence:

> Details: "the changes refer to exercising the right to vote, and cases where citizenship could be lost for different reasons; the widening and safeguarding of political rights for both the individual and political parties, which are to have free access to the media; freedom of speech, press, opinion, of education; (...) freedom of labor, of residence in any region of the republic, as well as to leave the country The use of public force is limited to the armed forces and the police (...)"
>
> (1970, Oct. 11. El Mercurio, p. 8)

The parliament approved the guarantees proposed by the UP and PDC (94 votes in favor versus 16 abstentions) (1970, Oct. 18. El Mercurio, p. 8). Finally, on Sunday, October 25, Allende was nominated president of Chile by the congress: 153 votes for Allende; 35 votes for Alessandri; 7 abstentions.

2 The Socialist Government of the Popular Unity Coalition (UP)

During the first year of government UP supporters were 'euphoric', whereas the right began the year 'demobilized and shocked' (Oppenheim, 1999, p. 54). In April 1971 there were municipal elections where the governing coalition got more than 49% of the votes (as opposed to the 36.2% in the presidential elections five months earlier). During that year the congress voted unanimously for the nationalization of the copper industry. The Agrarian Reform was continued and deepened as promised in the government's program.

The issue of the creation of a socialized sector in the economy generated much resistance in the opposition, and even within the governing coalition there were important disagreements about how to proceed. This made it impossible for Allende to pass a law on the expropriation of industries during the first year. However, he found a way around it. CORFO (the government's industrial agency) bought the majority of the stocks of some crucial financial institutions, thus effectively nationalizing the banks. The obvious limitation of this measure was the reluctance of the shareholders to sell their stocks to the government. The most striking case was the *Papelera* – the country's major paper industry. A large campaign against government control of this resource *("La papelera NO!!")* made it impossible for the government to buy it.

Politically, growing conflict within the UP coalition and between the UP and the opposition characterized the first year, though this conflict intensified and radicalized during the second and third year of the government. Because of the multi-party character of the governing coalition, a serious disagreement between moderate (Communist Party and Allende) and radical (faction of the Socialist Party) sectors made itself apparent. The moderate sectors wanted to stay within the constitutional limits and foster a majority for socialism. The radical sectors, on the other hand, wanted to move faster and favored popular mobilization to reach socialism.

At the end of the first year the government was starting to lose its momentum. The Christian democrats had leaned more towards the center (as opposed to the leftist orientation of the presidential candidate Radomiro Tomic), and the right had started to recover from its initial shock. It became openly oppositional and the far-right paramilitary group (Fatherland and Liberty, *Patria y Libertad*) started operating openly. By the end of 1971 the climate was of total confrontation.

In March 1972 there was a large-scale mobilization of women against Allende, known as the March of the Empty Pots and Pans *(la marcha de las cacerolas)*. The second year was characterized by an increasingly active opposition and obstruction of UP programs, which culminated at the end of 1972 in a merchants' and truckers' strike *(la huelga de los camioneros)*.

The economy had also deteriorated. Domestic production was unable to meet existing demand, nor could more imports be afforded. The US at that time cut all loans and credits to Chile, with the exception of its support to the military.

The big institutional dispute (between the executive and legislative) was still about the bill to socialize the economy. The PDC made changes to the president's initial proposal, Allende vetoed it, and the legislative claimed he had no power to do so. This constitutional debate, which might appear somewhat technical, was in fact a huge political problem. The divorce between the UP and the PDC was already a matter of fact.

The PDC and the National Party then created the Democratic Confederation [CODE] to campaign for the parliamentary elections in March 1973.

This political polarization was also reflected in the rest of society and conflict emerged between UP and opposition supporters.

In October 1972 there was a month-long national truckers' strike, making it impossible to transport basic food and other supplies to the capital because of the geographical features of Chile – long and very narrow. This strike is seen by analysts as a social, rather than political, mobilization of the Chilean middle class (Constable & Valenzuela, 1991). Many other sectors joined the strike and industries and businesses were shut down by their owners. For his part, Allende called on workers to 'defend' their workplaces and prevent industries from being closed. This large-scale mass mobilization acquired quite a violent character and exacerbated divisions in the Chilean population, between the opposition and the government, and between factions within the government itself.

The political crisis made Allende incorporate the hitherto unpoliticized military into the government with the appointment of General Carlos Prats as Minister for the Interior. Not all of the members of the UP approved of this development, with the Socialist Party being particularly against it.

In the aftermath of the strike in October, *JAP* (Price and supply associations) were created in order to ensure that the population would get basic supplies – a basket of basic goods which was made available to the population. Grocery store owners and the right in general saw this with suspicion, believing it to be a socialist measure to control food.

In 1973 there was still a 'legal limbo' regarding the issue of socialization of industries. In March 1973 there were parliamentary elections. Both the government and the opposition hoped the results would give creditability to their proposed politics. However, the lack of a clear electoral result continued to divide the country further. The election campaign was fierce. The opposition saw the elections as a plebiscite and called on the population to do so too. The center-right believed that their victory was essential to keep democracy in Chile and campaigned not only for the strong figure of the National Party (Sergio Onofre Jarpa, among others) but also for the need to 'replace the government'. The left presented the different voices of its coalition in the campaign; radicals called for 'Advance without Compromise', whilst the moderate sector used the slogan 'Consolidate and Keep Advancing'.

The election results gave the UP 43.5% of the popular vote, and the opposition obtained 56.6%. Both claimed victory. Compared to the presidential election results, Allende's coalition had indeed enlarged its popular support, though it had lost support when compared to the municipal elections of 1971.

3   The Emergence of a New (Violent) Political Articulation

Chilean political stability between 1938 and 1973 and the lack of radical antagonism between the right and the left relied on the exclusion of 'undisciplined' and 'anti-system' elements from the political field. The constitution of 1925, together with the immense repression that took place at the beginning of the century, managed to artic-ulate the otherwise 'anarchic' left within the limits of the political system. As histori-an Gabriel Salazar (1999) has described it, there was an agreement between the up-per classes and the *enlightened* lower classes. This agreement meant that the workers movement exchanged discipline for social and labor protection (and in this way, they distanced themselves from other existing popular expressions which were excluded from the political system). The right, on the other hand, although it held the presiden-cy only once during this period (1958–1964), positioned itself as the defendant of the stability of the law and Chilean social order.

This political order was threatened during the early seventies. The victory of the socialist candidate in 1970, the presence of new social groups that had not been pre-viously articulated – or disciplined – by the political system (women, agricultural workers, indigenous peoples, *pobladores*), as well as the growth of anti-system polit-ical rhetoric – which destabilized the legal identity of the left – definitively ques-tioned the viability of the identity of the existing political arrangement. The political became overwhelmed with 'non-political' elements which it was not able to include, since their exclusion, was at the basis of the possibility of its own existence. A new articulation came into being.

This new political articulation excluded the left this time, and 'the communist' be-came the condensed figure which represented what prevented Chilean society and politics from achieving complete fulfillment. The exclusion of the communist was to-tal and only its physical death could guarantee the stability of the new articulation. At the same time, there seems to be enough evidence to state that the left at the time was not able to crystallize its own new – non-legalist – articulation, but its elements re-mained closer to a state of dislocation. The new elements which overflowed the politi-cal did not manage to establish a chain of equivalency among themselves, but they kept competing for the establishment of a more radical form of politics (intended to declare themselves free from *legal constraints*). The presence of a new (violent) artic-ulation around the right, and the lack of a new leftist articulation produced an asym-metrical relation of antagonism between the right and the left during the early seven-ties which was expressed in the unilateral violence against the communist threat.

In their book *A Nation of Enemies*, Constable and Valenzuela (1991) very dramati-cally described the character of this unilateral war: the army was prepared to fight against a highly organized paramilitary society which, according to their view, would fight back against the coup. Instead they found no resistance whatsoever. In less than an hour, even the cities with the higher leftist votes where entirely at the mercy of the military forces. Moreover, in the days following the coup many civilians voluntarily gave themselves up after their names appeared on lists of people to be interrogated. They never thought they would not come back alive.

4   Historical Fantasies in Chile

The discursive elements of the definition of the political identity of the right and the left during the early seventies were not entirely new, but they can be traced back to earlier definitions of their political identities. Of course, this would not be the expression of an essence of the identity of the right and the left but rather the expression of a deeply established national imaginary around the concepts of modernity and enlightenment (translated into the high respect for the constitution), as well as particular features of the identities of the right and the left during the last period of stable democracy before the coup (1938–1973).

The social and political conditions in which the right (during 19th century) and the left (in the early 20th century) defined their identities meant that they did not share the same fantasy structure and so they did not develop a symmetrical relation of antagonism. The right (in its conservative or liberal expressions) had, and had historically maintained, the attribute of universality. The conservative right in particular considered itself to be the guarantor of social order and the moral good of the country (Cristi & Ruiz, 1992). For the left on the other hand, though inspired by a universal and antagonistic doctrine (Marxism-Leninism), universality and antagonism were not solid and stable attributes of its identity structure. This can be explained by its – at least partial – identification with liberal-republican notions of electoral politics and democracy (Puccio, 1988) and its early participation (1938) in wide governing coalitions. The attributes of universality and antagonism, therefore, remained instead as the *place* from where they saw themselves (and self-criticized) as rather reformist. The presence of this seeming contradiction in the left is an element that favored the distrust, which, as I have previously argued, was a crucial element in the emergence of antagonism.

a)   The Right

Since the beginning of the century, and mostly through historiography, Chilean thinkers such as Edwards (1982), Encina (1911), Eyzaguirre (1957, 1967), Lira (1974) and Guzman (1969, 1979) have produced a consistent (though not homoge-

neous) critique of liberal democracy and favored instead more aristocratic and authoritarian types of political organizations (Ruiz, 1979, 1981; Cristi, 1986, 1990).
Their claim was distinctly more moral than political; the need to restore the moral order. Their claim became political, however, when to their eyes such moral restoration
seemed viable only through political action of the right. Conservative historiography
actually seems to be the best testimony of what has been called here universality – the
possibility of identifying the stability of their particular identities (in this case, the political right) with the stability of Chilean society in general (Cristi & Ruiz, 1992).

From the very dawn of the Chilean republic and throughout the 19th century, the
major political contest was between conservative and liberal factions within the ruling oligarchy (Collier & Sater, 1996). This was a fight that underwent several 'revo-
lutions' and a civil war in 1891 (Jobet, 1971, 1995). The result was positive for the
liberals, who achieved a parliamentary system of representation, which, at the beginning of the 20th century, already incorporated new social sectors into political life.

The advances of liberal ideas first, and the deepening of democracy later, were
highly resented by the intellectuals and historians of the time. They painted Chilean
society as *decadent* (Palacios, 1904) and *inferior* (Eyzaguirre 1957, 1967) and
blamed the aristocracy for giving up the moral character of Chilean society (Edwards, 1982). Notions of historical continuity (based on theology or history), authority, order and tradition were the main ideas deployed by conservative thought to
resist the advances of liberalism and then of democracy. Their discontent led to military intervention in 1924, when the liberal president, Arturo Alessandri, was re-
placed by a right-wing *junta*.

In the writings from the beginning of the century the 'unavoidable' character of violent intervention to restore social order already existed, and has been described by
contemporary historians (Cristi, 1986, 1990) as a *conservative-revolutionary* type of
thinking; the moral vacuum calls for 'Caesarism', and Caesar can only be provided
by those capable of seeing the moral degeneration of society: the conservative right.

This same type of rhetoric can be found right after the coup of 1973, in the military's first official communications to the population (called *bandos militares*),
which gave the military an ideological, programmatic and informative referent. ...
*"That there exists in the country anarchy, asphyxia of liberties, moral and economic
insanity (...). That the Chilean population should trust the holders of truth and
morality (...). That the young population more than anybody else should trust their
destiny to the military forces who are taking care of them (...), and that acts of
resistance would be punished (...). That those who disobey these instructions will
suffer the rigor of Military Justice"*, etc. (quoted by Garretón, 1998). A year later,

the military regime put its *Declaration of Principles of the Military Government 1974* into circulation. This document condensed the main thoughts of the intellectuals mentioned above into a nationalist, corporativist and neo-liberal ideological synthesis.

b) The Left

On the left there was acceptance for the political legality crystallized after the revolution of 1891 and the constitution of 1925 (Moulián, 1988). This means that instead of attempting to destroy the bourgeois political order, it formed a part of it. Politically, this meant divorce between the workers movement and other existing popular organizations. "(…) between the enlightened people and the barbarians (…). This allows us to suggest that towards 1900, both the upper classes, as well as the enlightened from below, came together in a tacit alliance, in favor of the disciplining and order of Chilean society" … (quoted by Salazar & Pinto, 1999). This was the beginning of what is termed the *Estado de Compromiso*, where hostility was exchanged for political recognition and social protection. This meant a radical change in the way social and political struggles took place during the second half of 19th century and the first decade of the 20th. Inspired by the Russian revolution, the national union of workers had declared itself *anti-system*, but the new legislation divided the movement and some of its members (the Communist Party) decided instead to join the system. Certainly it was not only the presence of a new piece of social legislation, but also several massacres that took place in 1905, 1906 and 1907, and the repression of the last of the anarchist elements by Carlos Ibáñez, that inhibited the use of violence as a means of political struggle.

The claims of the left were partial rather than universal and could be paraphrased as 'wanting to reach social emancipation within the limits of the political emancipation already achieved'. It is possible to say that the left in the late thirties was already 'bound' to a symbolic order which made it establish a relation of *difference*, but not necessarily of *antagonism*, with the right. The first Marxist political organization was the Socialist Workers Party (*Partido Obrero Socialista* [POS]), founded and inspired by the ideas of Emilio Recabarren during the first decade of the 20th century. As described by Varas (1988), Recabarren's interpretation of Marx and Engels led him to believe in the need to foster universal suffrage and a wide, cross-class mass movement. One of the fundamental aspects of the political strategy of the POS was the use of legal mechanisms to increase popular power – 'there are only two forces: the law and the strike'. Though the bourgeois state would not transform the laws to protect the proletariat, Recabarren expected a parliament that represented the interest of the workers to be able to do so.

The electoral and coalition-based politics of Chilean communism led to accusations by the Latin American Secretary of the Communist International in 1926 that it was "a political aberration and deviation from the International" (Gómez, 1985). In 1938 the PC was already part of a large governing democratic coalition and formed part of it during three consecutive governmental periods (1938–1946). After a short interruption in Chilean democracy (1946–1952), the PC kept the same political strategy of wide electoral coalitions (Bascuñán, 1990).

The Socialist Party, on the other hand, was founded in 1933 and declared itself independent from the Communist International. This party was characterized throughout the period by its recurrent internal divisions because of ideological disagreements, and the presence of strong charismatic leaders, or *caudillos* (Moulián, 1983). Certainly the Socialist Party proved to be much less 'bound' to the principles of political liberalism than the PC. As is well known, in 1932 there was an attempt to build a socialist republic, though it only enjoyed a very ephemeral existence (under its great hero Colonel Marmaduque Grove). Thirty years later (in the party congresses of 1965 and 1969), and under the influence of the Cuban revolution, the PS seriously questioned its participation in electoral politics and voted instead for the *via armada* (armed solution). Given the unviable nature of such an option, the PS decided once again to join a wide coalition with the secular center and the PC and compete in the presidential elections in 1970 under the Socialist candidate, Salvador Allende. This decision was the source of yet another division within the party, and a small revolutionary party was founded (MIR). During the entire period of Popular Unity government (1970–1973) the party never solved its internal dispute and the president was highly criticized for its respect for the law and his understanding of the 'Chilean way to socialism' (Allende, 1972).

Considering the presence of ideological disputes it is fair to say that the Socialist Party would have liked to be able to position itself within a *universal* and *antagonistic* discourse but its historical attachment and participation in party politics and coalitions made this impossible. Chilean leftist legalism is indisputable. This also applies to the Chilean transition to democracy (where negotiation rather than rupture brought democracy back to Chile) (Schmitter, 1986). At this point it is important to mention that the presence of universality and antagonism might have given the right justification for military intervention. However, the coup was not only a transitional government or a short interruption in existing democratic life. This actually explains why the political center supported the coup: it shared the dimension of *antagonism* with the right but not that of *hate*. The Christian Democrat Party declared its opposition to the military regime as early as 1975.

In any case, a certain degree of historical continuity in the identity of the right and the left can be claimed not only from sources of political historiography but also from sociological findings. Though studies on violence in Chile show the existing relationship between the increase of votes for the left and the increase of violence in the country (Martínez, Tironi & Weinstein, 1990; Salazar, 1990), they also show that this was not physical violence against people (less than 3% of violent events resulted in death during violent acts from 1949 to 1988) but the expression of civil disobedience. The paradigmatic example of this type of violence can be found in the Agrarian Reform, where there was no physical violence against land owners, but *symbolic* violence. Violence organized by the right (in the twenties, late forties, and particularly in the decade of the seventies) was characterized by its literally fatal consequences.

During the years that preceded the coup in 1973, and particularly after the left won the presidential elections in 1970 (with only 36% of the votes), the other three attributes – antagonism, sexuality and hate – were added to the right's constant self-attributed universality. The left, on the other hand, at the time was facing the consequences of its historical *identity crisis* (the unsolved contradiction between its revolutionary and reformist character), which emerged as a lack of unity and consensus within the government (Moulián, 1983).

Chapter 7: Metaphors of Hate

Through a discourse analysis of the press coverage of the Chilean presidential elections in 1970 and the parliamentary elections in 1973, in this chapter I will analyze the symbolic construction of the figure of 'the communist' as an enemy of Chile that preceded the violence that occurred in September 1973.

As we will see, between 1970 and 1973 there was a clear displacement from the more discursive dimensions of fantasy *(universality* and *antagonism)*, to the more libidinal ones *(sexuality* and *hate)*. In 1970 the struggle between the right and the left was mostly *ideological*, where the right presented itself as being able to provide Chile with a better society (free, peaceful, modern, etc) than the left, which was seen as inspired by a violent and totalitarian foreign ideology. Under these circumstances, communism was fought in 1970 in a highly religious tone but by 1973 the political struggle was more *existential* than ideological. The right was not only fighting communism, but was fighting for the survival of Chile as a country. The enemy was not only the communist militant (portrayed in 1970 as lacking morality and individuality) but a Chilean 'mob' which was destroying the country and its people, for the 'pure pleasure' of it just to satisfy their base instincts. Under the Socialist government, they argued, Chileans would unleash a primitive self that threatened the very existence of the country.

In 1970 there was still room for negotiation but by 1973 distrust was total and words had entirely lost their meaning and permeability. There was only space for actions. Who would act first? In this context, the right saw itself as the only savior of Chilean society. Their view was that if they did not intervene (violently), Chile would disappear. Violence and hatred would consume the country.

1 The Content of the Political Propaganda

a) Universality: Social Order or Chaos and Disintegration

As previously stated, this dimension describes the way in which the stability of the whole society is equated to the stability of one particular identity. This equation provides the identity with a moral discourse that legitimizes its violence against the other. In the case of Chile, this first dimension of fantasy was presented in the press as a choice between social order or chaos and disintegration, so what was contested from the beginning of the seventies was not a particular political program but a basic understanding of Chilean morality. This moral dispute in 1970 was portrayed as a choice between morality/democracy and chaos/indoctrination. By 1973, however, this dispute was between peace and social disintegration. What is interesting to mention here is that in both cases there was almost no reference to concrete political programs, which is related to the fact that the political right was fighting against a 'spirit' that was seen as gradually poisoning the country. This gave the campaign a highly religious tone, where the soul of Chile was seen as being rescued from atheist Marxism. The position of the church at the time was crucial for the political right to be able to present such a discourse with legitimacy:

Let us consider the declaration of Chilean Bishops (1970, Sept 26):

> *"The Chilean people want to continue with their regime of freedom which has struggled for 160 years. They want the freedom of thought, the freedom to share ideas and to gather in organizations to be maintained and defended, and they want this freedom to grow and improve still more. (...) It is a fact that fear has taken over in Chilean families. There is fear of sudden changes, of mistakes, of unemployment. Fear of dictatorship, of compulsive indoctrination, of the loss of nation's moral and spiritual heritage."*

(El Mercurio, p. 25.)

The right's candidate, Jorge Alessandri, had to be invested with great symbolic power and was always associated with the great heroes of Chilean history and international personalities. He was portrayed as transcending worldly politics. Alessandri appeared to be an older, wiser man who would only become president because Chile needed him, not because of his personal or political aspirations.

Quotes by Alessandri (1970, El Mercurio):

> *"I will put an end to violence, terrorism and anarchy ...*
> *I only agreed to be a candidate because the political programs of the two other candidates will keep the country dancing to the tune of politicking and demagogy. That's why my main objective is to change the constitution and stop this from happening. (...) I will use an iron hand to stop the anarchy and the lack of social order that exists in this country, and to deal with those that promote violence, terrorism and crime."*

(Aug 22, p. 31.)

Alessandri's supporters (1970, El Mercurio):

> *"Alessandri stated that he wanted to cure the country of the bad political habits that are distorting and weakening democracy. He renewed his promise to establish an austere government, free from pressures and to fight against inflation."*

(Aug 16, p. 25.)

As can be seen from the quotes, the basic chain of equivalency of meaning here is Alessandri – Order – Rationality – Manhood – Peace – Chile. As a good, 'authoritative father', Alessandri's emphasis was on defending the law and putting an end to chaos. Another characteristic of the presidential campaign of 1970 was that it was mostly defined in negative terms (anti-Allende, anti-Marxist, anti-communist) and, as already stated, the right's political program was narrowly defined in terms of 'bringing back social order to the country' through a constitutional reform that would concentrate power in the office of the president.

In the next quote this confrontational character is clear; the option is either Chile or Marxism (1970, Aug, El Mercurio):

> *"In order to stop those who are destroying the moral values and awakening hate among people. we cannot make a mistake, because our error might be definitive. Through a long and hard struggle, humanity achieved the security of human rights. Respect for the human person, the freedom to think and express our thoughts, freedom of movement, the freedom of vocation and work, etc. The right to choose is what makes the difference between a freeman and a slave.*
>
> *Let's defend our right to keep choosing.*
>
> *We know that in communist countries there are no political elections. Their people cannot choose their lifestyle, or their government.*
> *Marxism, called communism, socialism, or 'Castrism', far from being an advance in achieving social wealth, is a violent backward process reverting to the beginning of civilization, since it wants to ignore what humanity has conquered through the centuries. It is imposed by hate and maintained by fear.*
>
> *Its best weapon is deceit. They offer to share it all, when in reality there will be only one owner: the state; they lie when they talk about peace, shattering the attempts at freedom of those people who live under Marxism with tanks. Those countries are only big prisons, where even poets pay for their free thoughts. (...)*
>
> *No real Chilean who knows this truth can choose Marxism for Chile. But some do. They use all weapons, even destructive and barbaric violence. They respect no serious Chilean institution or person. (...)*
>
> *But here in this free country, they won't succeed. Chilean women will not allow it. Jorge Alessandri has promised us that we women will have greater opportunities and safety. We call on all the women of Chile to defend the sovereignty of our country and its republican life, in this crucial moment of our history."*
>
> (p. 12.)

Though the political right always claimed to be 'apolitical' (precisely because its claims were *universal*), in 1973 their discourse was radicalized and the major clash shifted to 'evil politics versus upright military'. Indeed one of the elements present in the right-wing campaign against the socialist government was the call for the military to intervene and save Chile from the chaos that was dominating it. Authority

versus anomie and morality versus base passions were the main elements of the pro-military discourse. Discursive devices that were prominent in the military regime post-1973 were already present in the 1973 parliamentary election.
(1973, Feb 3, El Mercurio):

> *"Choose Labbe – a soldier not a politician!*
> *(...) Labbe is a soldier with vision, a man that knows his people, that knows our reality. Ours and ours alone. He stands for unity without foreign symbols. Labbe is order and justice!*
>
> *Labbe means austerity.*
> *A man educated in the army lives by moderation in his acts. A colonel is austere, responsible and serious"*
>
> (p. 24).

b) Antagonism: The Marxist other will destroy the country

This dimension describes the denial of the possibility of negotiation. As has been previously explained, antagonism (or the presence of a radical other) is constitutive of society (Laclau & Mouffe, 1985), but violence only emerges when combined with other elements of fantasy. The first discursive feature analyzed previously shows how the right positioned itself as the only moral savior of the country while establishing equivalency between itself, Chile and high moral standards. This second feature of antagonism clearly shows how communication and understanding between the right and the left was shattered. It was simply not possible for the political right to trust the left: 'their ideology is foreign and their acts are violent'. The political context of the sixties (characterized in Latin America by populism, land reform and guerrilla movements in neighboring countries), made the right 'deaf' to the words of the left. Any form of dialogue or understanding and, more importantly, the trust necessary to communicate with each other had already vanished. The legalism that the socialist government promulgated (the 'Chilean way to socialism') and the actual constitutional guarantees that President Allende was requested to sign before he could be nominated head of state meant nothing to the right who considered everything a 'lie'.
    Here are some examples:

> *"Allende lies:*
> *Mr. Allende, you have declared yourself to be a Marxist. But for Marxism, art must be at the service of its people, and fulfilling this doctrine, it has imprisoned, killed painters, writers, composers, etc. because they have expressed freely their ideas in those countries dominated by communism.*
> *So why do you say that if you become president you will respect artistic and cultural creation?*
> *Why are you mocking the Chilean people?*

"Political Plurality and Opinion Plurality:
The political parties that form the coalition that expects to govern the country (Popular
Unity) have repeated that they have no intention of constructing a Marxist regime, but a
political combination where ideological plurality will be fundamental. (...). Though the so-
cialist political leaders might have the best intention of keeping freedom alive, they will
end up restricting it, or suppressing it, because their vocation is totalitarian. They aim to
eliminate the ideas that obstruct or make it difficult to achieve their political purposes. (...)
The plurality of opinion is in itself contrary to Marxism. (...). Once they are in power those
aspects they have changed will appear again."

(1970, Sept 27, El Mercurio, p. 27.)

From the outset the right's relationship with the left had been antagonistic so from Allende's nomination as the first socialist president of the country to the day of the coup,
it was a matter of the growth and spread of anxiety, fear and hate. A large part of the
Chilean public also began to feel that the symbolic effectiveness of words and actions
was disappearing, to the point that this anomie was felt as a matter of life or death.

Part of this was expressed in the fact that the political right could not distinguish
the Chilean left from the international communists. For them it was all the same: Che
Guevara, Russia, Fidel Castro, East Germany and Salvador Allende. That is why it
made no difference what the president himself said about the particular character of
the 'Chilean way to socialism', which was at least formally characterized by respect
for existing legality.

In the 1970 campaign, the right defined its political opponents using these associations of meaning: Marxist – Foreign – Chaos – Evil – Failure – Mob. Let us look at
these definitions more closely:

Chaos and Violence:

The most common association that was constantly made in the newspapers was between Marxism and violence. Apart from the open fear of changing the basic values
of Chilean society (such as freedom, traditional family values and individual rights),
the major fear was the destruction of Chile as a country. Social conflict was a recurrent theme. There were many articles with big headlines about strikes, labor conflict,
land workers' conflicts: "72 hour-strike in health services" appeared on the same
page as "peasant conflicts continue ..." next to pictures of elderly people waiting for
their pension money which had been withheld for two months. Further on, on the
same page another article appeared about the rise in the cost of living and inflation
(1970, Aug 8, El Mercurio, p. 33).

What should be remembered here is that in 1970 there was a clear distinction between the contingent situation of the country (always portrayed negatively) and the

more permanent and positive 'Chilean spirit and high values'. Chile had already been in 'the wrong hands' for a while: a Christian democrat had been president for six years, and he had worked hand in hand with the left. The distinction between political contingency and permanent Chilean values became blurred in 1973 as badness came to be seen no longer as depending on bad leadership. Chilean values were perceived as changing: the Chilean people were no longer the same.

A few weeks before the presidential elections, the negativity became even more accentuated. The following appeared in a summary of the previous week's news:

> *"General Information:*
> *Agriculture: important losses due to peasants strike"; "Explosives and weapons belonging to the MIR found"; "More violent events" (Different terrorist attacks took place last week. In Iquique unknown persons tried to burn down the house of a navy officer; in La Union, an explosive went off and destroyed a newsstand ...) "Death in the snow" (a helicopter crashed in the snow and everybody died); "Strikes", etc.*

(Aug 9, p. 3.)

> *"Hundreds of pieces of land in the hands of peasants."*

(Aug 9, p. 43.)

> *"Marxism is incompatible with Andean Economic incorporation."*

(Aug 15, p. 25.)

> *"Agriculture: damage and activism."*

> *"Unrest, and in some cases, violence, reigns in numerous agriculture areas of the country. For a moment there were 199 tracts of land in the hands of conflictive peasants, lead by ultra-leftist leaders."*

(Aug 16, p. 25.)

Democratic Chile versus authoritarian Cuba:

A second permanent association conveyed was between Marxism, foreign doctrine, and the loss of sovereignty. In the editorials of August 1970 there were two recurrent topics: firstly, criticism of the idea of setting up a socialist experiment since 'democracy is not an experiment but a historical asset'; and secondly, the idea that it was 'irresponsible' to use utopian jargon when referring to social problems. All this was accompanied by the self-critique Fidel Castro had made openly earlier that year.

> *"Chile cannot be condemned to follow Cuba's example:*
> *Chile cannot be condemned to that certain day when Mr. Allende or Mr. Tomic have to recognize, as Fidel Castro did, that his revolution has failed, that there is only chaos, and that worse famines will come in the next ten years ...*
> *That's why Chileans will give the majority of their votes to Jorge Alessandri, 'Don Jorge'."*

(Aug 1)

As previously stated, the link between Salvador Allende and Fidel Castro received a lot of press cover. Full pages showed large pictures of Castro: "Promoters of Cuban revolution in Chile" accompanying a long article about the history of the Cuban revolution, and the way Allende and other left-wing political leaders had referred to it and welcomed it. The main purpose of the article however, was to provide information about the new agreements reached by the Latin American left in Havana: "The armed revolution constitutes the fundamental line of the Latin American revolution", or "the guerrilla, as the embryo of the liberation army, is the most effective means to initiate and develop the revolutionary process in the majority of our countries", and lastly, "the Cuban revolution, as the symbol of the triumph of the revolutionary movement, constitutes the vanguard of the Latin American anti-imperialist movement. Countries that take up the armed struggle, as they advance on their revolutionary path, are also in the vanguard ..." (1973, Aug 2).

Not even economic relations with Cuba where seen positively. The Chilean Society for the Defense of Tradition, Family and Property, reacted badly when a right-wing leader from the private sector of the economy tried to establish economic exchanges with Cuba: "nothing that improves official or diplomatic relations with Cuba is good for our country, since it will certainly mean the promotion of the influence of that communist country on Chile" (1970, Aug 2, p. 47).

Economic Crisis:

The third recurrent topic in the campaign of 1973 was the economic crisis, characterized by increasing inflation and a lack of productivity that resulted in shortages of basic food supplies. A range of articles, from editorials analyzing the inept policies of the government to tragic-comic headlines about different production sectors, could be found on almost every page of the newspapers. Here are some of the headlines:

> *"Last stage of progress: The redistribution of poverty*
> *(...) and lastly, why would it matter to the country that there is an improvement in income distribution when according to the most recent economic study published by the Department of Economics of the Chilean University the per capita income decreased by 4.4% during 1972?"*

(1973, Feb 3, El Mercurio, p. 3.)

> *"Critical situation in Valparaiso: bakeries closed since they lack flour."*

(1973, March 3, El Mercurio, p. 38.)

> *"Coming soon – Student Torture*
> *This year it will no longer be possible to refer to the 'school period' but to 'school torture'*
> *(...). This is because there are no school supplies and the ones available are too expensive*

(...) in conjunction with the ENU (unified educational system) which aims to standardize children's minds, and which will restrict the child's spirit to the Marxist doctrine."
(1973, Feb 25, Tribuna, p. 5.)

"Lack of supplies in hospitals
Operations being cancelled because of shortages of basic medical supplies; minor surgery undertaken without anesthetic since there is lack of this basic element; two women per bed in the maternity ward, and in emergency cases even three women per bed ... "
(1973, Feb 4, El Mercurio, p. 1.)

"Massive bankruptcies of Chilean Companies"
(1973, El Mercurio, Feb 4, p. 34).

"30% of buses out of service due to lack of mechanical supplies"
(1973, Feb 17, El Mercurio, p. 30).

Destruction of basic Chilean institutions:

A fourth topic that became very prominent in 1973 was fear of the destruction of basic Chilean institutions. The judiciary, legislature and the police *(carabineros)* were all portrayed as threatened and losing their symbolic power and legitimacy, which created a strong fear of anomie. Pictures of police officers being beaten by leftist paramilitary groups appeared on the front page of the newspapers (Durán, 1995, p. 54).

"Popular Justice

Communism, as part of its purpose to destroy Chilean democracy, has maintained a permanent position of undermining the judiciary in order to destroy one of its fundamental institutions. Their leitmotiv is that justice must be applied by the people, as a popular, direct justice, without the intervention of courts and legal processes."

(1973, Feb 17, Tribuna, p. 5.)

"New Attacks Against the Judicial Power
Once again Montt Vargas Square was the scene of a belligerent protest between groups from the UP and the judicial power, this time caused by an eviction decision handed down by a judge in Santiago. Protesters called for the creation of people's courts (tribunales populares) instead of the ones that our constitution contemplates."
(1973, Feb 3, El Mercurio, p. 3.)

"UP militants shoot policemen
A serious gun battle took place yesterday night in Valparaiso between the police and extremists that had participated in an assault on the office of the PDC."
(1973, Feb 3, El Mercurio, p. 24.)

All this social disorder affected the possibility of keeping democratic institutions alive and, additionally, the 'morals' of the country were seen as fading away. Political disorder leads to social disorder. Bad leaders are followed by bad citizens. The country had become a nation of enemies.

c) Sexuality and Hate: Communists are Evil – they enjoy our suffering

The hyper-sexualization (or more generally the dehumanization) of the enemy characterizes antagonism in its libidinal dimension. When one of the identities steps outside morality strictures (and becomes violent) in order to 'defend' the morality that protects society, it fights against an enemy which is portrayed as evil. Sexuality and hate refer to the animalization of the other and the possibility of enjoying their suffering. Let us look at how this was expressed in the Chilean newspapers of the time:

> *"Murderous UP callousness:*
> *Each day the murderous callousness of the UP becomes clearer and more terrifying. The examples of their de-humanization are soaring and each one shows a greater decisiveness and desire to create unrest and anger, and to humiliate the Chileans."*
> (1973, Feb 25, Tribuna, p. 5.)

> *"New Victim:*
> *There is a new victim of the bestial and primitive hate preached from the highest spheres of the government – this time a child of 14, murdered by a shot to the head by members of the UP. (... The tree of hate has borne fruit. Those who eat of it need no prior provocation. Children are being killed and helpless women beaten only to satisfy base instincts and create fear ... "*
> (1973, Feb 10, Tribuna, p. 5).

The 'pernicious' acts of the left were explained as the result of their lack of morality and decency; they were seen as harming people only to satisfy their passions. Furthermore, it seemed that the suffering of others gave them pleasure. This demonization of the left was the result of a permanent association between the left, animality and homosexuality:

> *"The Great Chilean Line*
> *Chile has been transformed into a gigantic line of people that goes from Arica to Magallanes. Men and women of all ages have found themselves forced to stand in the most diverse lines to obtain what they need for their homes. What started as an ordered way of making beef available to all has been extended to almost every food supply.*
> *(...) However, some queues have disappeared altogether since some supplies are not available. This is the result of low levels of internal production in the country and the impossibility of importing the required goods ... "*
> (1973, Feb 11, Tribuna, p. 1.)

This is particularly interesting because of the association between anomie, animality and femininity. The Chilean expression for queue or line of people is *cola*, which also means 'tail', so it is interesting to see how Chile (under the UP government) is seeing as growing a tail. It is akin to saying: 'we are becoming so primitive (violent, anarchists), that we now resemble an animal'. The newspaper Tribuna used to refer to communists as *colas* (again, 'tails'), which also means homosexual in the local pejorative slang. The association between these terms is quite clear: Chile is becoming a homosexual country. As we will see later, this pejorative understanding of the country seems to be a crucial element in the overall justification and spread of violence.

The evil and success of the left are well expressed in the next quote:

> *"The Rape of Consciousness:*
>
> *There is a type of 'rape' which children and adolescents suffer, which is even worse than physical rape. This is moral or consciousness rape. Some parents aren't even aware of its existence.*
>
> *But there are indeed 'professional rapists' of consciousness. Maybe they even go through some sort of special education in order to learn how to do it. Their mission is to recruit children and young people in order to assure the continuity and expansion of their political party fanaticism. They take them young so that they are unsuspecting. The result is that before they become adults, they are already fanatics and as such they don't want to hear anything which is outside their doctrinal framework. This kind of person, indoctrinated with totalitarian ideas, is basically a servant of the party. He would kill his own father if told to do so. He is just a being deprived of will and autonomy. He becomes a puppet, doing the bidding of the party.*
>
> *This is a person that is capable of anything if the party asks for it: treason, physical aggression, murder or genocide.*
>
> *It is sad to think that their parents dreamt of their becoming an honorable person."*
>
> (1970, Aug 9, El Mercurio p. 33.)

The campaign of the center-right coalition (CODE) in 1973 followed a similar logic to the presidential elections in 1970, with violence as its central topic. The repeated use of pictures of the dead, in particular in Tribuna, is remarkable. In this respect it is interesting to mention that there was a clear division of labor between the two newspapers: El Mercurio stressed the *symbolic* character of the loss of 'Chileanhood' (expressed in the economic, political and moral crises) whilst Tribuna stressed the *physical* character of the crisis (dismembered bodies intended solely to arouse fear of death).

The front page of El Mercurio, a month before the elections showed a large table giving statistics for violent acts in the previous 25 days (Feb 3, p. 1):

> *"25 Days of Violence*
>
> *Period covered between the 5th and 31st of January 1971:*
> *Detained*
>
> *For propaganda without authorization*
> *UP* *241*
> *Opposition* *208*
> *Total* *449*

For carrying guns
UP   6
Opposition   9
Total   15
For violent attacks
Against persons and offices of UP   12
Against persons and offices of opposition . . .   18
Total   30
Dead and wounded in fights, attacks and disorder
Dead   3
Wounded . . . .   41 "

What it is particularly interesting about this rather simple description of violent events, is that both right and left are portrayed as responsible. As we will see later, the spread of the propensity for violence, from the left to the rest of the population is a crucial element in the 'call' for the coup. It is not only the *other* but also the *self* who is part of this chaos.

The perception of this change in Chilean society was represented by the figure of Frankenstein. The lack of moral integrity in the government's leaders had awakened the worst in the Chilean people. The rhetoric of violence in 1973 was not only about political violence, but also about delinquency and criminality; social unrest, anarchism and anomie had invaded the streets, universities and workplaces. This feeling of fear only grew into terror after the UP launched its election campaign. The discourse of Salvador Allende, who led a big demonstration at the National Stadium, stated that the election was not a plebiscite, and that "in the end the electoral results were not all that important". The power of the people, he said, lay somewhere else, in "popular power". Allende called for the formation of revolutionary civic associations.

In a couple of editorials which appeared El Mercurio the focus on fear, not of the government, but of society emerged quite clearly. This 'popular power' incorporated not only the foreign, atheist and totalitarian doctrine, but, far worse, the whole 'Marxist mob' associated with the worst of the Chilean spirit; criminal, delinquent and anarchic.

What it is interesting about this is that a new division in Chilean society was being created between *real* Chileans (those who opposed UP) and those who supported the left-wing government. This same division was at the heart of Pinochet's discourse and practices during the years of the dictatorship.

After Allende's speech calling for revolutionary civil associations to be set up, fear also increased regarding the president's own commitment to the legalist 'Chilean way to socialism'.

"Our surprise increases when considering that the president has virtually eliminated the democratic path in his discourse when he states: 'now and after March 4th (day of the elections) workers know they have the CUT (Central Unico de Trabajadores), the peasant committees and the organizations of Popular Power'... 'the strength of the workers that rely not on the few (i.e. senators) but on the social force that they represent, and this is the base and mystique of popular government'. Allende had previously declared: 'the contest for the political direction of the country will not be decided on March 4th for the workers'. The result of the elections will not influence the politics of the government. According to the president, nothing will stop Marxist forces from constructing a parallel power to the constitutional authorities"

(1973, Feb 11, El Mercurio, p. 29).

Other headlines expressed the same fear:

"The president of the republic insists on launching 'the mob' against legislative power"

(1973, Feb 17, Tribuna, p. 7).

"Description of the New Man (Hombre Nuevo[28]):
In physical terms the New Man is no different from the classical one. He can be tall, short, healthy or weak. It is in the cultural and philosophical traits where his main characteristics permit zoological classification:
He is of a very narrow culture. He is a very dogmatic person. His horizon is limited. Only the present fits in his mind. (...) He is shy, aggressive, and a liar. Lazy and disaffected. Sadly disaffected."

(1973, Feb 25, El Mercurio, p. 55.)

Finally, it is important to stress the physical character of the anti-UP propaganda, which showed literal expressions of wanting to get rid of communists, not only by winning the parliamentary elections, but again literally by 'destroying them'. Several of the logos of the different right-wing candidates used either a hand or a foot smashing a UP symbol or breaking it into pieces.

---

[28] The idea of the New Man *(hombre nuevo)* is part of the left-wing rhetoric used in Latin America during those years which expresses the classic Marxist portrayal of unspoiled human nature that emerges once capitalism is defeated.

Chapter 8: The Meaning of Anti-Communism in Chile

In order to understand the cultural and social dimension of the violence that emerged in Chile in 1973 I have proposed to work with the notion of fantasy and I have mentioned universality, antagonism, sexuality and hate as its basic components.

As shown in the preceding chapter, the four elements that characterize violent fantasy were present in the anti-communist rhetoric of the political propaganda of the presidential and parliamentary elections of 1970 and 1973. The most salient ones were antagonism and universality. The left represented a mortal threat to the country *('nothing has been left intact, neither our economy nor our morals')* while the right was seen as the only force that could save the country *('Have you thought what would happen to Chile if the Partido Nacional did not exist?')*. At the end of 1972 the relation of antagonism had already been openly declared, and political negotiation between the right and the left no longer had any viable space. Discourse had lost its communicative power and distrust and hate had taken over instead. For the political right in Chile, a threat to its identity was seen as a threat to the moral identity of the country. It was a mortal threat not only to them as individuals, but to the whole of society too. Their enemies, the 'communists', were not only capable of taking their economic and political power from them, but also of taking the very soul of their society.

The political struggle and antagonism between the right and left was framed as a battle between good and evil. The right, defending the social order (and basics principles of morality), could become violent (amoral) in order to protect the social order ('good has to win to, no matter what'). Secure in its identity (as the holder of high moral standards), the political right could easily transgress the basic principles of its community without fearing the loss of such identity. Their amoralization was their transgression.

The legal (partial or non-universal) identity of the left fought against the bourgeois, which was a 'partial' enemy, not a mortal one. The left's view of the bourgeoisie cannot be compared to the right's view of the communists as an evil power. The bourgeois only incarnated the degeneration of a society, which could be improved. That said, the left also transgressed in defending the expansion of rights, it became 'illegal' (it transgressed the law), but not 'amoral' (it did not transgress basic social principles), when defending itself from the right. This (partial) transgression, accounts for the acts of *symbolic* violence described in previous studies (civil disobedience, protests, illegal occupation of lots, etc.).

The absence of violence against the bourgeoisie is the best testimony of the absence of a universal and antagonistic fantasy in the left.

The other two dimensions of fantasy – hate and sexuality – were also present in the political campaigns. This was expressed mostly in the amoralization and demonization of communists, who were always compared to animals guided by their instincts and lacking moral knowledge, or to worthless and irrational crowds. Regarding sexuality, in the two campaigns it was possible to see how the right used the language of the 'father' (of order, authority and rationality) against the 'feminine' passionate (anomic) language of the left. The Tribuna newspaper constantly referred to left wingers as *'miricones'*, producing a neologism from two words: *'mirista'* (belonging to the MIR, a revolutionary left grouping) and *'maricones'* (degenerates, homosexuals). As previously stated, they also often referred to them as *'colas'*, which has the same pejorative meaning. In this game of words and deeds, the military ended up being seen as ultimately authoritative men pitted against the politicians who could neither prevent nor stop social, economic and political disaster. This explains why the fear of destruction of legal and police institutions became so important; it seemed as if the left could also *kill the father*.

Anti-communism represented a variety of fears and hates. The first and most obvious was the opposition to the structural economic changes pursued by the socialist government, which meant the loss of property and social privilege. A second deeper fear was that of anomie. The legalist, orderly, friendly and rational country was turning into a passionate, chaotic and hateful place. Violence and animosity took over streets, workplaces and universities. The economy was sinking and an unknown mob was acquiring power.

But what did this anomie represent? My conclusion is that anti-communism at a certain point also expressed self-hatred or hatred for an aspect of Chilean identity. Hate against the communists was both a condensation and a projection of hate for a deeper, wilder Chile – an aspect of the country's identity that the elites had attempted to eradicate for an entire century. In a country like Chile, anomie is particularly painful because the country had embraced modernity and rationality so strongly and proudly, whilst being an under-developed country. The findings of my research indicate that the social, economic and political chaos that the country had experienced since the late sixties, though initially seen as the product of bad political leadership, was later perceived as the consequence of an amoral public. The 'people' of Chile had become a sinister monster (described as a Frankenstein) capable of the worst crimes to satisfy their basest desires. The shift in the object of hate from the leftist political elites to the general public seems crucial in understanding the spread and character of the violence that emerged in 1973. The political fight (and subsequent repression) was not only against an imaginary well-organized red army, but also against a Frankenstein, or a malevolent Chilean spirit roused by the UP *("the tree of evil had borne its fruits")*. Chile was losing its civil, rational and modern structure, and a primitive society was being unleashed. *"Moral corruption of youth worsened by UP"* (1972, Sept 26, Tribuna, p. 1). This omnipresent spirit hid behind a faceless mob, but it crystallized in the amoral figure of the communist.

At the same time, it was difficult to decipher the figure of the president. Allende was seen as waking this monster but just who was Allende? A crazy, unfit, unaware fool leading bad, anarchic citizens? Or a cold-minded totalitarian? The first figure represents a president whose main problem was lack of power and authority over his political alliance and over his country. This is the image of a divided and impotent government/president that cannot prevent chaos. The country falls to pieces while the government/president discusses metaphysical issues *('sus entelequias')*. The second figure is entirely different and represents a very powerful person who has everything under control and is leading the country towards a totalitarian regime. The presence of these two quite different aspects in the character of the president (and the government) definitely helped the right to increase fear. They could not really answer the question *'who is Allende?'* or *'what does Allende want?'*, and that impossibility made them fantasize about him and his government as being the devil incarnate. Though Allende was a moderate within his party and had endorsed the legal construction of socialism, his general behavior and the erratic behavior of his government could only be read as the devil's hell; *"The UP is the Devil's Cauldron"* (1973, Feb 25, Tribuna, p. 3).

Finally it could be said that the relation of antagonism between the right and the left was already *physical* before the coup, not only because there were paramilitary organizations on both sides *(Patria y Libertad and MIR)* involved in physical clashes in the streets, university campuses and workplaces. Let us remember that the radicalization of the opposition between right and left in Chile had commenced with the Agrarian Reform, in which landowners felt betrayed by their land workers (and by their country which had allowed this to happen). The *'toma de fundos'* (expropriation of land to give it to rural land workers) was part of a large-scale leftist 'party' that was being celebrated in every rural region. At the same time it was experienced

by the right as the greatest tragedy and injustice that had ever happened in the country. This antagonism had already been physical to a certain extent since it had created
feelings of euphoria in the left and hate – expressed as aggressive jealousy – in the
right.

Death and suffering were already present in the social imaginary of Chile before
the coup. The repeated publication of pictures of dismembered bodies in the news,
bold headlines about horrible violent crimes, and the rather obvious images of the
left being 'smashed' by the right, had created a perverse background where death
was looked at with horror and, at the same time, excitement.

In summing up it can be said that the brutality of the violence not only aimed to repress left-wing political activists but also to extirpate a devil from the Chilean soul
that was destroying the nation, to punish a society for having allowed this to happen,
and to restore a patriarchal social order. The mixture of horror and excitement that
characterized the pre-coup Chilean press points to the paradoxical dynamic of
morality and enjoyment that characterized it. Violence was justified as a moral calling to rescue society from evil but, at the same time, it involved a perverse eroticization of death.

Conclusions

The question that has inspired this study is how in Chile, a country with a consolidated democratic tradition, a violent military dictatorship could emerge and remain in power for 17 years. As stated in the introduction of the book, political science has answered this question from a strategic point of view – the Chilean case corresponded to an example of well known bureaucratic military regimes, where the objective of violence and the production of fear in the population was to dismantle political activity and foster political apathy to allow the military to govern without opposition. Without ignoring the context of the cold war and the anti-communism that accompanied it, I have argued that strategy can only explain partially what happened in Chile. The best illustration to show the shortcomings of such interpretations is precisely the lack of strategic or rational elements in the violence that characterized the military regime.

At a theoretical level this question could be translated into another question about definitions of the self and the other that facilitate the emergence of violence in societies where the rule of law has been accepted as the legitimate means to solve conflicts (as was the case in Chile).

I have argued that existing studies of collective violence fall short in understanding the wild, non-strategic, nor culturally learnt character of collective violence, and that according to my view, this is the result of the lack of conceptualization of a structural rupture between the self and the other. I therefore analyzed the process of identity formation, looking for a theoretical perspective which would offer both a structural account of the rupture between the self and the other (where the other is theorized as a constitutive outsider) and the conceptual tools necessary to understand the wild (non-strategic) character of violence. In order to theorize this rupture, I proposed to work with the concept of radical otherness or the constitutive outsider, using Durkheim's notion of the sacred and Freud and Lacan's notion of the unconscious. The line of the argument is that any social identity, in order to exist, needs to exclude/repress something outside itself, and that what it excludes keeps destabilizing the constituted identity. Using Castoriadis's words, I stated that the social process follows a certain logic that has no clear resolution: society self-institutes itself but it denies its own invention for the sake of its stability. Denying its contingent character, society creates a *transcendent* or sacred narrative about its origin but this narrative fails to conceal the existence of a prior pre-symbolic and meaningless pure being, therefore, society keeps experiencing the threat which this abyss poses to the constitution of society.

The excluded other appears to be able to lift the thin veil of imaginary construction that covers the chaos and presents a threat to the stabilization and meaning of the identity. Violence emerges when the identity as such is threatened, when what is feared is the total loss of the symbolic titles which cover the prior – the asocial state of pure dislocation or anomie. Violence is thus existential.

So far we have dealt with the impossibility of the closure of the symbolic realm and the presence of a constitutive outsider. This non-closure is also manifested in the inter-subjective relation in the impossibility of full recognition. There is always a blank space, a margin of doubt about the other's desire: *"you are telling me this, but what do you really want?"* According to psychoanalytical theory, the excluded element is what escapes symbolization, what it is beyond language: the 'real', or pure, pulsing drive.

The ignorance about what the other wants brings us to fantasy. Using Zizek's work, it was argued that fantasy functions as a construction, as an imaginary scenario filling out the void, the opening of the desire of the other. The concept of fantasy was introduced to explain the double nature of the constitution of the social bond: the transcendental narrative not only establishes the law, it also frames desire: *what the law prohibits, (unconscious) desire seeks.*

The ethical claims about the restoration of social order, as well as ways of enjoying the exclusion of the other, are not gender neutral but in fact represent both male ethical claims (about the restoration of the threatened patriarchal order) and male forms of enjoyment. In our patriarchal society particular types of (gender/sexual) identities are fostered and those identities (feminine and masculine) are framed by a primarily masculine (or Oedipal) super-ego, or morality. Masculinity (transgression) and femininity *(jouissance)*, account for two different ways of enjoying in existing patriarchal societies (and not because of biological or social differences). The first one is characterized by the fact that men, being subordinated to symbolic castration, are caught within the symbolic order. Masculine enjoyment, therefore, consists of transgressing the symbolic order to reach the realm of the drives. For their part, women are not as exposed to the threat of castration as men are and are therefore not caught up entirely in the symbolic order, but also exist in the real (what is beyond symbolization).

Since what it is outside of the realm of the symbolic is what threatens the identity and produces violence as a response, the more feminine and less patriarchal the society, the lesser the experience and fear of social disintegration. In addition, the more feminine the society, the smaller the need to transgress the symbolic order in order to enjoy. Is this lack of transgression equivalent to a *status quo*? No. Using Weber's typology of religious rationality, I established a parallel between ascetic societies and male/transgressive forms of enjoyment; mystic societies and artistic/sublimating forms of enjoyment; and dualistic societies and feminine/*jouissance* forms of enjoyment. I argued that pure asceticism (transgression) opens up space for social antagonism while intervening in the world and eliminating the other as a threat. Pure mysticism (sublimation) on the other hand, while sublimating suffering does not express violence against the other which embodies a threat. However, their lack of intervention in the world makes mystic societies live in a quite violent form of social organization, since deep social inequality and lack of freedom would not be combated either (castes societies). I proposed then the model of dualism *(jouissance)*. Though this type of (feminine) identity is 'active' (it produces exclusion like all social identities), the constitutive outsider is recognized and is therefore less threatening for the stability of the identity. The result is that there is more inclusion and less antagonism (violence).

In summing up it can be said that the inclusion of a gendered, informed analysis allowed me to state that collective violence (at least in modern societies) not only seeks the restoration of social order, but the restoration – or reinforcement – of *masculine law* or patriarchal social order. Violence and exclusion are regarded here as expressions of a masculine way of enjoying transgression of the symbolic order, whereas the excluded other *par excellence* was defined as *feminine desire*, associated with passivity and disintegration in our masculine culture. Though democracy is less likely to produce violence than authoritarian regimes, it still can and it does create enemies. I argued for the incorporation of the dualist model of society as expressed in the theory of hegemony. I also argued that democracy not only needs to acknowledge the presence of a constitutive outsider but also the possibility of fostering different identity structures that relate with what they exclude in a different way, and the very physicality of social relations.

My case study allowed me to argue that a violent fantasy is characterized by the presence of four elements: universality, antagonism, sexuality and hate. Universality refers to equating the stability of society to the stability of at least one of the particular identities involved in a relation of antagonism. In doing so, the self takes on a moral discourse of privileged moral knowledge that legitimizes its violence against the other. Antagonism refers to the denial of the possibility of negotiation. Sexuality expresses the relation of jealousy of enjoyment: *'your enjoyment is my misery'*. This dimension is expressed in the amoralization, or hyper-sexualization, of at least one of the identities. It is experienced as disgust for the other's way of enjoying.

When one of the identities steps outside morality (and becomes violent) in order to 'defend' the morality that protects society, it fights against an enemy which is portrayed as evil; an enemy which has to be eradicated. Hate refers to the possibility of at least one of the parties enjoying the suffering of the other.

I have argued that these four dimensions of violent fantasy were present in the press coverage of the parliamentary and presidential elections of 1970 and 1973 respectively. This means that the political conflict in Chile went beyond ideological frontiers and entered an existential and physical terrain even before the coup. The findings of my study point to the fact that communism not only represented a foreign, totalitarian doctrine which some Chilean political and social sectors resisted fiercely, but that anti-communism at a certain point also represented the imminence of chaos and destruction of the moral basis of the country. The perception was not (only) that the Chilean left was leading the country to communism but to anarchy. Moreover, communists were seen as lacking human values: they were destroying the country and its people only to satisfy their base instincts. As I have attempted to show, from 1970 to 1973 there was a significant shift in meaning in traditional anti-communism and also in distrust, fear and hate, which changed its focus from militants to the rest of society. The people of Chile had become a sinister monster (described as a Frankenstein) capable of the worst crimes to satisfy their base instincts. I argued that the displacement of hate from the leftist political elites to the general public is crucial in understanding the spread and character of the violence that emerged in 1973. This society did not just need to be saved – it needed to be punished.

Moreover, I have also argued that anti-communist hatred could be interpreted as a condensation and projection of self-hatred; hatred towards a *wilder deeper feminine Chile* – an aspect of the country's identity that for an entire century elites (and middle classes) had attempted to erase. In a country like Chile anomie is particularly painful because it had embraced modernity so strongly and proudly whilst being an under-developed country.

Selected Bibliography

Aldunate, Adolfo et al. Estudios sobre el sistema de partidos en Chile. Santiago de Chile: FLACSO, 1985.

Alexander, Jeffrey. Twenty Lectures. New York: Columbia University Press, 1987.

Allende, Salvador. Pensamiento Poliitico. Santiago de Chile: Editorial Quimantú, 1972

Althusser, Louis. "Ideology and State Apparatus". Mapping Ideology, ed. by Slavoj Zizek. New York: Verso, 1994.

Apter, David. The Legitimization of Violence. New York: New York University Press, 1997.

Arato, Andrew, and Eike Gebhardt. The Essential Frankfurt School Reader. New York: The Continuum Publishing Company, 1994.

Austin, J.L. How to do things with words. Cambridge, Mass: Harvard University Press, 1962.

Badiou, Alain. Ethics: An Essay on the Understanding of Evil. New York: Verso, 2001.

Bailey Gill, Carolyn. Bataille: Writing the Sacred. New York: Routledge, 1995.

Barthes, Roland. Elements of Semiology. New York: Hill and Wang, 1964.

- Mythologies. New York: Hill and Wang, 1998.

Bascunan, Carlos. La Izquierda sin Allende. Santiago de Chile: Editorial Planeta, 1990.

Bataille, Georges. Eroticism, Death and Sensuality. San Francisco: City Lights Books, 1986.

- Visions of Excesses, Selected Writings. Minneapolis: University of Minnesota Press, 1994.

Benjamin, Jessica. Like Subjects, Love Objects: Essays on Recognition and Sexual Difference. New Haven: Yale University Press, 1995.

- Shadow of the Other. Intersubjectivity and Gender in Psychoanalysis. New York: Routledge, 1998.

Blumer, Herbert. Symbolic Interactionism: Perspective and Method. New Jersey: Prentice Hall, 1969.

Bourdieu, Pierre and Loic Wacquant. An Invitation to Reflexive Sociology. Chicago: The University of Chicago Press, 1992.

Bourdieu, Pierre, Language and Symbolic Power. Cambridge, Massachusetts: Harvard University Press, 1994.

Bowie, Malcom. Lacan. Cambridge, Massachusetts: Harvard University Press, 1991.

Borch-Jakobson, Mikkel. Lacan, The Absolute Master. Palo Alto: Stanford University Press, 1991.

Bracher, Mark. Lacan, Discourse and Social Change. A Psychoanalytic Cultural Criticism. Ithaca: Cornell University Press, 1993.

Braunstein, Nestor. Goce. Santiago de Chile: Editorial Siglo XXI, 1990.

Butler, Judith. "Contingent Foundations". On Feminist Contentions. Ed. by Linda Nicholson. New York: Routledge, 1995.

– The Psychic Life of Power: Theories in Subjection. Palo Alto: Stanford University Press, 1997.

– Excitable Speech: A Politics of the Performative. New York: Routledge, 1997.

Butler, Judith, Laclau, Ernesto & Zizek, Slavoj. Contingency, Universality and Hegemony, New York: Verso, 2000.

Calhoun, Craig. Habermas and the Public Sphere. Cambridge, Massachusetts: MIT Press, 1996.

Castoriadis, Cornelius. World in Fragments. Palo Alto: Stanford, 1996.

– The Imaginary Institution of Society. Cambridge, Massachusetts: MIT Press, 1998.

Collier, Simon, and William Sater. A History of Chile, 1808–1994. Cambridge: Cambridge University Press, 1996.

Collier, David. The New Authoritarianism in Latin America, Princeton University Press, 1980

Collins, Randall. Four Sociological Traditions: Selected Readings. Oxford: Oxford University Press, 1994.

Constable, Pamela and Arturo Valenzuela. A Nation of Enemies: Chile under Pinochet. New York: W.W. Norton, 1991.

Cooke, Maeve. Habermas: On the Pragmatics of Communication. Cambridge, Massachusetts: MIT Press, 1998.

Copjec, Joan. Read my Desire. Cambridge, Massachusetts: MIT Press, 1995.

– Radical Evil. New York: Verso 1996.

Copjec, Joan. Supposing the Subject. New York: Verso, 1994.

– Imagine There is no Woman. Ethics and Sublimation. Cambridge, Massachusetts: MIT Press 2003.

Cornell, Drucilla et al. Deconstruction and the Possibility of Justice. New York: Routledge, 2000.

Cristi, Renato & Carlos Ruiz. El Pensamiento Conservador en Chile. Santiago de Chile: Editorial Universitaria, 1992.

Cristi, Renato "El Pensamiemto conservador en Chile 1903–1974". Revista Opciones. Santiago de Chile, 1986.

– "Comunitarismo y Liberalismo." Revista de Ciencia Politica. Santiago de Chile, 1990.

Critchley, Simon, and Peter Dews. Deconstructive Subjectivities. Buffalo: State University of New York Press, 1996.

Culler, Jonathan. On Deconstruction: Theory and Criticism after Structuralism. Ithaca: Cornell University Press, 1982.

Dayan, Daniel and Elihu Katz. Media Events: The Live Broadcasting of History. Cambridge, Massachusetts: Harvard University Press, 1992.

Debray, Regis. The Chilean Revolution: Conversations with Allende. New York: Pantheon Books, 1972.

Dews, Peter. The Limits of Disenchantment: Essays on European Philosophy. New York, Verso 1995.

– Logics of Disintegration. Post-Structuralist Thought and the Claims of Critical Theory. New York: Verso, 1987.

Doanne, M.A. et al. Re-Vision. Los Angeles: The American Film Institute, 1984.

Dollard, John et al. Frustration and Aggression. New Haven: Yale University Press, 1939.

Dor, Joel. Introduction to the Reading of Lacan. New Jersey: Bookmart Press, 1997.

Ducrot, Oswald. Le Dire et le Dit. Paris: Minuit, 1984.

Duran, C. El Mercurio: Ideología y Propaganda 1954–1994. Santiago de Chile: Cesoc, 1995.

Durkheim, Emile. The Division of Labor in Society. New York: The Free Press, 1984.

– The Elementary Forms of Religious Life. New York: The Free Press, 1965.

Elster, Jon. The Cement of Society. Cambridge: Cambridge University Press, 1989.

Edwards, Alberto. La Fronda Aristocratica en Chile. Santiago de Chile: Editorial Universitaria, 1982.

Elliot, Anthony. Psychoanalytic Theory: An Introduction. Durham: Duke University Press, 2002.

Encina, Francisco. Nuestra Inferioridad Economica. Santiago de Chile: Editorial Universitaria, 1911.

Eyzaguirre, Jaime. Historia de las Instituciones Politicas y Sociales de Chile. Santiago de Chile: Editorial Universitaria, 1967.

– Ideario y Ruta de la Emancipación Chilena. Santiago de Chile: Editorial Universitaria, 1957.

– Fisonomia Historica de Chile. Santiago de Chile: Editorial Universitaria, 1973.

Fink, Bruce. A Clinical Introduction to Lacanian Psychoanalysis. Theory and Technique. Cambridge, Massachusetts: Harvard University Press, 2000.

– The Lacanian Subject: Between Language and Jouissance. Princeton: Princeton University Press, 1995.

Foucault, Michel. History of Sexuality Vol. I. New York: Vintage Books, 1978.

– Discipline and Punish. New York: Vintage Books, 1979.

Freud, Sigmund. Totem and Taboo. New York: Norton, 1950.

– Group Psychology and the Analysis of the Ego. New York: Norton, 1959.

– Introductory Lectures to Psychoanalysis. New York: Norton, 1989.

– The Ego and the Id. New York: Norton, 1960.

– The Interpretation of Dreams. New York: Basic Books, 1965.

– Civilization and its Discontents. New York: Norton, 1961.

Friedman, Reinhard. 1964–1988: La Politica Chilena de la A a la Z. Santiago de Chile: Melquíades, 1988.

Garber, Marjorie et al. The Turn to Ethics. New York: Routledge, 2000.

Garfinkel, Harold. Studies in Ethnomethodology, Prentice Hall, 1967.

Garreton, Manuel Antonio. Por la Razon y sin la Fuerza: Analisis y textos de los bandos de la dictadura militar. Santiago de Chile: LOM, 1998.

Giddens, Anthony. Central Problems in Social Theory – Action, Structure and Contradiction in Social Analysis. Berkeley: University of California Press, 1979.

Gomez, J. Ese Cuarto de Siglo. Santiago de Chile: Editorial Andres Bello, 1985.

Goldhagen, Daniel. Hitler's Willing Executioners: Ordinary Germans and the Holocaust. New York: Vintage Books, 1997.

Gramsci, Antonio. Selections from Prison Notebooks. New York: International Publishers, 1961.

Grosz, Elizabeth. Jacques Lacan: A Feminist Introduction. New York: Routledge, 1990.

Gurr, Ted Robert. Why Men Rebel. Princeton, NJ: Princeton University Press. 1970.

Guzman, J. "El Miedo. Sintoma de la realidad politico-social chilena." Revista Portada 2. Santiago de Chile, 1969.

– "El camino politico." Realidad 7. Santiago, 1979.

Habermas, Jürgen. The Structural Transformation of the Public Sphere. Cambridge, Massachusetts: MIT Press, 1962.

– Theory of Communicative Action. Cambridge, Massachusetts: MIT Press, 1984.

– On the Logic of Social Sciences. Cambridge, Massachusetts: MIT Press, 1967.

– The Inclusion of the Other. Cambridge, Massachusetts: MIT Press, 2001.

– Between Facts and Norms. Cambridge, Massachusetts: MIT Press, 1998.

– Moral Consciousness and Communicative Action. Cambridge, Massachusetts: MIT Press, 1999.

– On the Pragmatics of Communication. Cambridge, Massachusetts: MIT Press, 1998.

– Knowledge and Human Interests. Beacon Paperbacks, 1972.

– "Civil Disobedience: Litmus Test for the Democratic Constitutional State." Berkeley Journal of Sociology (1985): 95–116.

Halperin, Thomas. The Contemporary History of Latin America. Durham: Duke University Press, 1993.

Hansen, Beatrice. Critique of Violence: Between Poststructuralism and Critical Theory. New York: Routledge, 2000.

Honneth, Axel. Struggle for Recognition. Cambridge, Massachusetts: MIT Press, 1996.

Horkheimer, Max and Theodor W. Adorno. Dialectics of Enlightenment. New York: Continuum Publishing Company, 1997.

Howarth, David. Discourse Theory and Political Analysis. Manchester: Manchester University Press, 2000

Human Rights Watch. Los Limites de la Tolerancia: Libertad de Expresion y Debate Público en Chile. Santiago de Chile: LOM, 1998.

Husserl, Edmund. Cartesian Meditations: An Introduction to Phenomenology. The Hague: Martinus Nishoff, 1960.

Irigaray, Luce. This sex which is not one. Ithaca: Cornell University Press, 1977.

Jocelyn-Holt, Alfredo. El Peso de la Noche: Nuestra frágil fortaleza historica. Buenos Aires: Editorial Ariel, 1997.

– El Chile Perplejo. Santiago de Chile: Editorial Planeta, 1998.

Joas, Hans. Pragmatism and Social Theory. Chicago: The University of Chicago Press, 1993.

– The Creativity of Action. Chicago: The University of Chicago Press, 1996.

Jobet, Julio Cesar. Ensayo Critico del Desarrollo Economico y Social de Chile. Santiago de Chile: Editorial Universitaria, 1995.

– El Partido Socialista en Chile. Santiago de Chile: Editorial Planeta, 1971.

Jonassohn, Kurt and Karin Solveig Bjornson. Genocide and Gross Human Right Violations in Comparative Perspective. Somerset: Transaction Publishers, 1998.

Jullien, Philipe. Jacques Lacan Returns to Freud. New York: New York University Press, 1994.

Katzenstein, Peter. The Culture of National Security: Norms and Identity in World Politics. New York: Columbia University Press, 1996.

Kelly, Robert et al. Hate Crime: The Global Politics of Globalization. Illinois: Southern Illinois University Press, 1998.

Klein, Melanie. Envy and Gratitude. New York: The Free Press, 1975.

– Love, Hate and Reparation. New York: Norton, 1964.

Kojeve, Alexandre. Introduction to the Reading of Hegel. New York: Basic Books, 1969.

Kornbluh, Peter. The Pinochet File: A Declassified Dossier on Atrocity and Accountability. The New Press, 2003.

Kristeva, Julia. Revolution in Poetic Language. New York: Columbia University Press, 1984.

– Powers of Horror. New York: Columbia University Press, 1983.

Kristeva, Julia. Strangers to Ourselves. New York: Columbia University Press, 1991.

– The Language of the Unknown. New York: Columbia University Press, 1989.

– Desire in Language. New York: Columbia University Press, 1980.

– El Genio Femenino: Melanie Klein. Buenos Aires: Paidos, 2000.

Lacan, Jacques. Ecrits. New York: Norton, 1977.

– Freud's Papers on Technique: Seminar Book I. New York: Norton, 1991.

– The Ego in Freud's Theory and in the Technique of Psychoanalysis: Seminar Book II. New York: Norton, 1991.

– Four Fundamental Concepts of Psychoanalysis: Seminar XI. New York: Norton, 1978.

– On Feminine Sexuality: The Limits of Love and Knowledge. Seminar XX. New York: Norton, 1998.

– The Ethics of Psychoanalysis: Seminar VII. New York: Norton, 1997.

Laclau, Ernesto and Chantal Mouffe. Hegemony and Socialist Strategy. New York: Verso, 1985.

Laclau, Ernesto. Emancipation(s). New York: Verso, 1996.

– The Making of Political Identities. New York: Verso, 1994.

Linz, Juan and Alfred Stepan. The Breakdown of Democratic Regimes: Crisis, Breakdown and Reequilibrium. Washington, DC: John Hopkins University, 1978.

Lira, Osvaldo. "Nacion y Nacionalismo." Pensamiento Nacionalista. Ed. by Enrique Campos. Santiago de Chile: Gabriela Mistral, 1974.

Lira, Osvaldo et al. Psicologia de la Amenaza Politica y del Miedo. Santiago: ILAS, 1991.

Loveman, Brian et al. Las ardientes cenizas del olvido. Via chilena de reconciliación politica 1932–1994. Santiago de Chile: LOM, 2000.

Lyotard, Jean Francois. The Postmodern Condition: A Report on Knowledge. Minneapolis: University of Minnesota Press, 1979.

Marcuse, Herbert. Eros and Civilization. Boston: Beacon Press, 1955.

Martinez, Javier & Tironi, Eugenio. et al. Personas y Escenarios en la Violencia Colectiva. Santiago de Chile: Ediciones SUR, 1990.

Marx, Karl. The Marx and Engels Reader. Ed. by Tucker. Princeton: Princeton University Press, 1978.

Mead, George Herbert. On Social Psychology. Chicago: The University of Chicago Press, 1977.

– Mind, Self and Society. Chicago: The University of Chicago Press, 1967.

MIDEPLAN. "Evolución de las Políticas Sociales en Chile, 1920–1991." *Documentos Sociales*, Santiago de Chile, 1991.

Mouffe, Chantal. The Return of the Political. New York: Verso, 1993.

– The Challenge of Karl Schmitt. New York: Verso, 1999.

– The Democratic Paradox. New York: Verso, 2000.

– Deconstruction and Pragmatism. New York: Routledge, 1996.

Moulián, Tomás et al. Discusiones entre Honorables. La Derecha en Chile 1938–1946. Santiago de Chile: FLACSO, 1985.

– Democracia y Socialismo en Chile. Santiago de Chile: FLACSO, 1983.

– "Evolucion Historica de la Izquierda Chilena. Influencia del Marxismo." FLACSO *Documento de Trabajo N. 139*. Santiago de Chile.

– "Continuidad o Cambio en la Línea Política del Partido Comunista de Chile?" *El Partido Comunista de Chile*. Ed. by Varas. Santiago de Chile: FLACSO, 1988.

– Conversación Interrumpida con Allende. Santiago de Chile: LOM, 2000.

Münch, Rainer. Sociological Theory Vol. 1, 2, and 3. Nelson-Hall, 1994.

Munizaga, G. et al. El Discurso Publico de Pinochet 1973–1978. Santiago de Chile: FLACSO, 1983.

Nunn, Frederick. The Military in Chilean History: Essays on Civil-Military Relations 1810–1973. Albuquerque: University of New Mexico Press, 1976.

Olson, Mancur. The Logic of Collective Action. New York: Schooken Books, 1968.

O'Neill, John. Hegel's Dialectic of Desire and Recognition. Buffalo: State University of New York Press, 1996.

Oppenheim, Lois. Politics in Chile: Democracy, Authoritarianism and the Search for Development. Westview Press, 1999.

Palacios, Nicolas. La Raza Chilena. Valparaíso, 1904.

Parsons, Talcott. The Structure of Social Action. New York: The Free Press, 1937.

– The Social System. New York: The Free Press, 1951.

Parker, Andrew et al. Nationalisms and Sexualities. New York: Routledge, 1992.

Poole, Deborah et al. Unruly Order: Violence, Power, and Cultural Identity in the High Provinces of Southern Peru. Westview Press, 1994

Puccio, Osvaldo. "La Politica del Partido Comunista de Chile. Elementos de su evolucion y permanencia." El Partido Comunista de Chile. Ed. by Varas. Santiago de Chile: FLACSO, 1988.

Ramirez-Necochea, Hernan. Balmaceda y la Contrarrevolución de 1891. Santiago de Chile: Editorial Universitaria, 1972.

– Historia del Movimiento Obrero en Chile. Antecedentes Siglo XIX. Santiago de Chile: Editorial Lar, 1986.

Reyes Matta et al. La Prensa: Del Autoritarismo a la Libertad. Santiago de Chile: CERC, ILET, 1989.

Ricoeur, Paul. Hermeneutics and the Human Sciences. Cambridge: Cambridge University Press, 1981.

– Freud and Philosophy: An Essay on Interpretation. New Haven: Yale University Press, 1970.

Ritzer, George. Frontiers of Social Theory: The New Synthesis. New York: Columbia University Press, 1990.

Ruiz, Carlos. "Tendencias Ideologicas en la historiografia chilena del siglo XX." Escritos de Teoria (1979). Santiago de Chile.

– "On Authoritarian Ideologies in Chile." Canadian Journal of Latin American and Caribbean Studies 6 (1981).

Sagaris, Lake. After the First Death: A Journey Through Chile's Time Mind. Toronto: Somerville House, 1996.

Salazar, Gabriel & Pinto, Julio. Historia Contemporanea de Chile. Santiago: LOM, 1999.

Salazar, Gabriel et al. Personas y Escenarios en la Violencia Colectiva. Santiago: Ediciones SUR, 1990.

Salecl, Renata. "Hate Speech." Radical Evil. Ed. by Joan Copjec. New York: Verso, 1996.

– Sexuation Sic 3. Durham: Duke University Press, 2000.

– The Spoils of Freedom: Psychoanalysis and Feminism after the Fall of Socialism. New York: Routledge, 1994.

– Gaze and Voice as Love Objects. Durham: Duke University Press, 1996.

Sarup, Madan. Poststructuralism and Postmodernism. Athens: University of Georgia Press, 1988.

Saussure, Ferdinand. Course in General Linguistics. New York: McGraw-Hill, 1959.

Scarry, Elaine. The Body in Pain. The Making and Unmaking of the World. Oxford: Oxford University Press, 1985.

Schmitt, Carl. The Concept of the Political. Chicago: The University of Chicago Press, 1996.

– The crisis of parliamentary democracy. Cambridge, Massachusetts: MIT Press, 1994.

Schmitter, Philippe et al. Transitions from Authoritarian Rule: Latin America. Washington, DC: John Hopkins University Press, 1986.

Sigmund, Paul. The Overthrow of Allende and the Politics of Chile 1964–1976. Pittsburgh: University of Pittsburgh Press, 1977.

Sintesis Informe Rettig. Nunca Mas en Chile. Santiago de Chile: LOM, 1999.

Smelser, Neil. Theory of Collective Behavior. New York: The Free Press, 1962.

Suau, Fernando. La Democracia en el PDC Chileno: 1957–1970. Santiago de Chile: Editorial Andres Bello, 1989.

Subercaseaux, Bernardo. Historia de las Ideas y de la Cultura en Chile. Santiago: Editorial Universitaria, 1997.

Sunkel, Guillermo. El Mercurio: 10 anos de difusion politica e ideological 1969–1979. Santiago de Chile: Estudios ILET, 1983.

Stavrakakis, Yannis. Lacan and the Political. New York: Routledge, 1999.

Swidler, Ann "Cultural Power and Social Movements", in Hank Johnston and Bert Klandermans (eds.), Social Movements and Culture. Minneapolis: University of Minnesota Press, 1995.

Taylor, Charles et al. Multiculturalism: Examining the Politics of Recognition. Princeton: Princeton University Press, 1994.

Thompson, John. Ideology and Modern Culture. Palo Alto: Stanford University Press, 1990.

– The Media and Modernity. Palo Alto: Stanford University Press, 1995.

Theweleit, Klaus. Male Fantasies. Minneapolis: University of Minnesota Press, 1987.

Tilly, Charles, From Mobilization to Revolution. New York: McGraw Hill, 1978.

Urzúa, Germán. La Democracia Práctica: Los Gobiernos Radicales. Santiago de Chile: CIEDES, 1987.

Varas, Augusto. "Ideal Socialista y Teoria Marxista en Chile." *El Partido Comunista en Chile.* Ed. by Varas et al. Santiago de Chile: FLACSO, 1988.

Verhaeghe, Paul. Does the Woman Exist? From Freud's Hysteric to Lacan's Feminine. London: Rebus Press, 1999.

Valenzuela, Arturo. The Breakdown of Democracy in Chile. Washington, DC: John Hopkins University Press, 1978.

Vidal, H. Chile: Poetica de la Tortura Politica. Santiago de Chile: Editorial Setenta & Tres Press, 2000.

Weber, Max. Economy and Society. Berkeley: University of California Press, 1978.

– From Max Weber: Essays in Sociology. Ed. by Hans Gerth and C. Wright Mills. New York: Oxford University Press, 1958.

Weitzel, Ruby. Tumbas de Cristal: Libro Testimonio de la Vicaria de la Solidaridad. Santiago de Chile: Cesoc, 1991.

Whitebook, Joel. Perversion and Utopia: A Study in Psychoanalysis and Critical Theory. Cambridge, Massachusetts: MIT Press, 1996.

Wood, Elisabeth Jean. Insurgent Collective Action and Civil War in El Salvador. Cambridge University Press, 2003.

Yocelevsky, Ricardo. La Democracia Cristiana Chilena y el Gobierno de Eduardo Frei (1964–1970). Mexico-City: Universidad Autónoma Metropolitana, Unidad Xochimilco, 1987.

Zizek, Slavoj. The Sublime Object of Ideology. New York: Verso, 1989.

– The Plague of Fantasies. New York: Verso, 1997.

– The Fright of Real Tears. London: British Film Institute, 2001.

– The Metastasis of Enjoyment. New York: Verso, 1994.

– The Ticklish Subject: The Absent Center of Political Ontology. New York: Verso, 1999.

– On Belief. New York: Routledge, 2001.

– Cogito and the Unconscious Sic2. Durham: Duke University Press, 1998.

Newspapers:

El Mercurio

Tribuna

VS Forschung | VS Research
Neu im Programm Soziologie